31 DAYS
to EXCEL *in*
BUSINESS

T0349350

31 DAYS
to EXCEL *in*
BUSINESS

LIFE TOOLS
FOR SUCCESS

LARRY WINGET

MEDIA

MEDIA

Published 2025 by Gildan Media LLC
aka G&D Media
www.GandDmedia.com

Front cover design by David Rheinhardt of Pyrographx

Designed by Meghan Day Healey of Story Horse, LLC.

Library of Congress Cataloging-in-Publication Data is available upon request

ISBN: 978-1-7225-0707-7

10   9   8   7   6   5   4   3   2   1

Contents

INTRODUCTION   7

CHAPTER 1
31 Days to Being Customer Focused   9

CHAPTER 2
31 Days to Getting Along with Others   43

CHAPTER 3
31 Days to Getting What You Want   77

CHAPTER 4
31 Days to Leadership   111

CHAPTER 5
31 Days to Making More Sales   145

CHAPTER 6
31 Days to Success!   179

Introduction

There are thousands and thousands of books about success, goal setting, sales and more. Chances are high that you've read several of them. I sure have. And I have written my share of them and even sold quite a few, hitting several bestseller lists along the way. Most all the "how to be more, do more and have more" books are pretty good at laying out the end game of success in various areas. And while the end game is indeed what we are all looking for when we decide to change our life and results, looking at the end game is short-sighted. Yep, short-sighted. Because keeping your eyes focused only on the end game is a sure-fire, guaranteed way to make you get tripped up along the way.

Your life and results are the way they are, good or bad, because of the dailyness of your thoughts and actions. If you are overweight, you didn't get there overnight. You got there because every day you did things that led you to that result. If you want to lose weight, it won't happen overnight either. It will take daily changes. Same for your finances, your relationships and every other aspect of your life and business. You got where you are because of what you did daily.

That's what this little book is all about: the dailyness of better results. Things you can do every single day to make today a little better than yesterday and tomorrow a little better than today. Success (and failure) is the cumulative effect of daily changes. Here I give you daily changes you can make to achieve better results. None of them are earth-shattering changes. Chances are you've heard everything I suggest many times before. Good. Consider these simple suggestions a solid reminder of all the small changes you can make every single day so you can finally get what you want. Don't rush. Don't say, "Yeah, sure, I do that already." Take your time, be thoughtful about each day and move forward with determination and awareness.

Now, get going!

CHAPTER 1

31 Days to Being Customer Focused

What It Means

To be customer focused is to put the customer first at all times. It means that you have to look at what you do and how you do it through the eyes of your customer. You have to focus all of your efforts of satisfying the customer through your products and services and how you offer those products and services.

Each individual and each job function, even entire departments and companies, must move forward to serving the customer in every way. You must serve through your sales efforts, through your customer service efforts, through your collection efforts, leadership and advertising. Customer service is no longer a department. Each person must take responsibility. When the entire organization is focused on better serving the customer, then the entire organization will be rewarded by receiving the business of the customer.

The principles of being customer focused will work equally as well for your internal customers, too. You have to serve co-workers and other departments in the same ways you would serve a customer on the outside.

Day Two

The Three Reasons Every Person Should Go to Work Every Day

These three reasons will give you a simple set of priorities for you and your organization. They are:

1. To keep existing customers
2. To create new customers
3. To make yourself and your organization the kind that people want to do business with

Look at everything you do and make sure that your activities fall into one or more of these priorities.

You'll find this to be a great decision-making tool as well as an effective time management tool. When it comes down to doing either A or B or spending your time doing this or that, then look at the list. If it accomplishes one of these things, then it is a good decision and a good use of your time.

You and your organization will become much more customer focused if you remember to constantly be doing things that keep the customers you currently have, create new customers, and make you and your organization the kind that people want to do business with.

Day Three

Keeping Existing Customers

You have to do everything within your power to retain your current customer base. They are your surest source of income to your business and are the greatest source of referrals for new business. Never sacrifice your existing base of customers in order to get new customers. You aren't building the business at that point, you are trading customers. Besides, it costs approximately five times more to get a new customer as it does to keep the one you've got.

Existing customers are familiar with you, your company, your products and services and your procedures. As creatures of habit, customers can become very loyal to an organization. If listened to and treated right, they will buy more often than will new customers. It will be easier to get them to try new things you offer and even to trade up to more expensive services. And they are your company's best salespeople. Many times the mistake is made of focusing on new business without putting the ones we already have in the right priority. And that priority is number one!

Day Four

Create New Customers

Some would say that the job of creating new customers is the job of the sales department. The responsibility of creating new customers is everyone's job. Every person within your organization must be a salesperson. Every person while on the job and off must develop the attitude of serving others by offering your products and services.

To be a good salesperson, you have to become aware of the needs, wants, desires and concerns of others. And just being aware and sensitive to those issues will allow you to more easily recognize opportunities to put your products and services within those organizations and into the hands of those people.

So right now, begin to think of yourself as a salesperson. Help others within your company to think of themselves as salespeople. Learn how to better offer your products and services to people at any time you recognize a need and know you have a solution. Help other employees to be able to do the same.

Nothing happens until something is sold.   —RED MOTLEY

Day Five

Make Yourself And Your Organization The Kind People Want To Do Business With

Customers like to do business with people, not places. Building and maintaining relationships is one of the keys to being customer focused. Make sure that you are the kind of person that someone would want to build a relationship with. Think about the kind of people you like to do business with. I'll bet they are friendly, punctual, accessible, presentable, knowledgeable, nice folks. I'll bet they are honest and have integrity and are trustworthy. These are the qualities for an outstanding person. Spend time making sure that you are this kind of person, not just at home and with your friends, but with your internal and external customers.

These same qualities apply to organizations, too. Customers want to be able to say that they are proud to business with you and your company. Make sure that you are that kind of person and company. Focus on your personal and professional development.

Day Six

Know Your Boss

All of us in business have a boss. As a salesperson, you have a sales manager. As a clerk, you have a supervisor. Even as the company president, you have a board of directors. And the board of directors has shareholders. Everyone has a boss.

But more importantly, you all have a boss who is in total control of your success. That boss is the customer. This boss is the one who gives your organization money for the products and services you provide. And if they go away, everyone can go home! It's over! So, it's up to you to concentrate on pleasing the ultimate boss, the customer, as much and in as many ways as possible. The more you are able to please the boss, the more likely the customer will do business with you and share their money with you and your organization. This is what allows the business to survive and grow, and gives each person within the company job security and a better environment to work within.

Day Seven

Love Your Boss

What!? Yes, love your boss. Love the people who come in the door. Remember, if they don't come in, you get to go home. Forever. If you will put the customer first, understand that the customer pays your salary and all of the expenses to keep the business running, and is responsible for your personal and professional success, you will find it much easier to love the customer: the boss.

What I mean by love is appreciation, respect, courtesy and the willingness to serve. Loving your boss simply means developing an attitude of sincere thankfulness toward the customers for allowing you to serve them and for trusting you with their business. Let them know that you really care and that you are glad to see them and that you want to do everything you can to help them. It's very important to go well beyond just knowing who your boss is. You must develop the right attitude and learn to love your boss.

Day Eight

Love Your Boss's Problems

It is said that being successful in business is finding a problem and solving it. So the more you are faced with problems, the more opportunities you will have to be successful. Problems are the key to your significance. You demonstrate your knowledge, creativity, and worth by solving problems.

Loving problems means you love success. The more you love a problem, the more able you will be to overcome, work through, and resolve the issue at hand. It is your love for the problems that actually allows you to be more creative in finding solutions to your customers' problems. This will work whether you are in a fast food restaurant or in the most high-tech, high-dollar business in America. Customers bring you their problems, expecting you to have something that will solve that problem. So learn to love that problem. Have a passion for finding and delivering the solution. Become solution-oriented, understanding that all of your solutions are developed to meet and exceed the customers' expectations.

Day Nine

Take Responsibility

One person can make the difference. Even when an entire organization doesn't agree on focusing on the customer, one person who is in touch with the customer can have a powerful impact on whether that person comes back and tells others about your business. Conversely, if the whole organization has made a decision to be customer focused and one employee does not take responsibility for meeting and exceeding the customer's needs, the customer will perceive that the entire company doesn't care. One flight attendant can determine whether you will ever fly that airline again. One person at that fast food restaurant will influence your decision to ever visit that chain again anywhere in the country.

Regardless of the size of the company, it's up to the individual. If you understand that a customer is doing business with the people in the company and not the company, then it is critical that each person take responsibility for demonstrating customer focused service. This in turn will create an image of your company as a customer-oriented organization. One person does make the difference.

Day Ten

Be Nice

If all of the money you are ever going to have is currently in the hands of someone else then it is important to understand the major principle in getting them to share that money with us. Be real nice! Did you ever give your money to someone who wasn't nice to you? Of course you did. But I bet you didn't do it more than once. And that's because we have a choice: a choice to do business with people who are nice to us. That is part of the third reason for going to work every day: to make sure that we are the kind of people that others want to do business with. People want to do business with people who are nice. This simply means caring about the other person. If you are sincerely nice, then you will smile, you'll be courteous, and you'll listen. The good news is that it really doesn't take any longer to be nice than rude. And it takes very little energy. And the best part is that you will see instant results. Angry customers won't be able to stay angry and happy customers will want more than ever to share their money with you.

Day Eleven

Be Proactive

It is easier to be nice to people if they are nice to you. But sometimes the customer is not very nice. In fact, sometimes they are pretty rude and even mean. So it is best to gain some skills that will allow you to stay in control of the situation. The best skill is to be proactive. Determine that you want nice, friendly, easy-to-get-along-with customers and show that same attitude to them. If you take a proactive stance and start every relationship with a smile, a friendly face and an attitude of willingness to help the customer, it is more likely that you will get the positive response back from them that you want. If you take a reactive position and let the customer take control of the relationship, then you will find yourself at a disadvantage. Sometimes you'll find yourself in a negative situation desperately trying to salvage the relationship and the customer.

So take the lead. If you want someone to smile at you, then smile at them first. If you want nice customers, and we all do, then be nice. Give your customers an example to follow. Be the kind of person that you would like to have as a customer.

Day Twelve

Be Flexible

No two humans are alike. Therefore, no two customers are alike. They may come to us with the same problem, particularly if we are in the kind of business that has a narrow focus. But the way they communicate that problem will be different, the type of solution they need will be different, and how they use or apply the solution you offer will be different.

So in order to solve the problem of each individual customer, even if it's the same problem every time, you have to be flexible enough to meet their individual needs. You need to be able to adjust your language, listen to them as though you are experiencing the problem from their point of view, and understand what solving the problem really means to them.

Customers are people first and customers second. They all come to you with their individualities and their uniqueness. You can't deal with everyone the same way if you really want to be customer focused. Super success comes through the special treatment for every individual.

Day Thirteen

Be Empathetic

Meet the customer where they are. This means to have empathy for the customer. Not sympathy. Sympathy says I feel like you do. That is impossible. There is no way that you can duplicate the feelings of another person. However, you can have empathy. Empathy says I understand how you feel. Try to understand why customers feel the way they do.

This is important because customers can be very myopic when it comes to their problem. If they could see beyond the problem to solutions, then they would be much easier to get along with. In order to help them see solutions, you have to start where they are and carefully lead them toward the solution you have to offer.

While your knowledge of your product and service is greater than theirs, their knowledge and understanding of the problem is greater than yours. So empathize with the customer to get into their shoes and understand why they are feeling and acting the way they are. Only then can you really communicate your solution and your ideas so they will understand. This is one of the keys to true customer satisfaction.

Day Fourteen

Be Reliable

Be the kind of person your customer can count on every single time. Work to make your company the kind that the customer can count on every single time.

This means being dependable, with consistency. Let customers know what they can expect from you every time you do business with them. Consistent quality of products and services is the number one indicator of a successful organization. And it's easy to understand why. Consistently performing in an excellent manner builds trust. When customers trust you, they will be loyal to you and refer others to you. There won't be any need for them to shop around. Because they are getting what they want from you every time.

Think of the time you tried that new restaurant and it was great. And then the next time you tried it, it wasn't any good at all. Because of the inconsistency, you probably won't go back. You have too many other choices. Your customer has choices too. Make sure that you are reliable. Make sure that you and your company can be counted on every time.

Day Fifteen

Be Punctual

As a customer focused person and organization, being punctual doesn't just mean being on time. It means that you respect the customer's time more than you do your own. You place the customer's time at the top of your priority list. Whether you go to them, they come to you, or even if they are on the telephone, the customer is giving up some of their precious time for you. This is an opportunity for you to prove to them just how valuable they really are to you.

If you are calling on a customer, this means you have to be right on time for the appointment. If the customer comes to you, then you have to jump to wait on them or to help them. Move quickly, and serve them as quickly as you can without compromising quality and without rushing the customer. When customers call you on the telephone, they want your undivided attention. If it is impossible at that moment to give it to them, ask if you can call them back. In all cases, respect the customers' time. That's the one thing that they can never get back.

Day Sixteen

Be Available

Make sure that the customer understands that you and your organization are there for them when they need you and for as long as they need you. Be available, accessible and willing to talk with them and provide service when they need it.

Make sure you have enough telephone lines coming in so the customer can get right through and not get busy signals. And make sure you have someone there to answer the phones when they ring. This sends a signal to the customer that you are available for them. If you personally aren't there for them when they call, then make sure that the person answering the phone can get a message to you or that you pick up your messages promptly. The customer should know when they can expect you to return their call. And you should return their call!

Being available means that when you are with a customer, that you are with that customer. Give them your attention. Avoid interruptions. Avoid telephone calls and talking with other people during your time with the customer. Be there for them with your undivided attention.

The more available and accessible you are, the more customers will want to reward you with their business.

Day Seventeen

Be Decisive

Customers are looking for someone to solve their problems. They are not necessarily looking for all of the alternatives you may need to consider, or all of the research you may need to do, nor do they want a dissertation on all of the knowledge you may possess on the subject. They want an answer. Give your customers answers. Let them know whether you can fix the problem or whether you will need help. Then get help. Show decisiveness. If you can't prove to the customer that you can make a decision, then very likely they will take their problem to someone who can. At that point, you have lost out.

Decide first that you will do the thing that moves you closer to meeting and exceeding the customer's expectations. Decide if you can or have the ability to fix the problem and then tell the customer. Even if it takes time, or if you have to go to someone else for help, if you are decisive then the customer will have a feeling that you are a person who gets things done! That will build confidence and trust in you and your organization.

Make a decision to be the best and do the best for the customer at all costs!

Day Eighteen

Look Good

People gather information 87 percent by sight. By appearances. So you gotta look good! You have to look at yourself and your company through the eyes of your customer. Appearances are important. If you don't look good then there is a very good chance that you will never get an opportunity to prove to the customer that there is more than meets the eye.

Customers will judge the quality of your service and your ability to meet and exceed their expectations more by how you look than the product and service that you actually provide. How would you feel if you got on an airplane that had dirty tray tables? Would you question how the engine looked? Sure you would! Look around your business. Or have a friend come over and tell you how it looks. If your office looks disorganized, shoddy or dirty, customers will make up their mind that's the kind of service they will get too. Is that fair? Sure it is! They are the customer! And the customer can never be wrong. So look good all of the time!

Day Nineteen

Ask

In order to deliver customer focused service your goal must be to meet and exceed all customer expectations. Here is the problem. Most of us just don't know what the customer expects. We go about making the assumption that we know what they want. What if you don't? So what do you do? Ask. You have to ask the customer what they expect from you. When you know, you can meet and exceed their expectations.

People love to give you their opinions. So ask them, and I promise they will tell you. And you want them too! No matter how ugly it may be.

So ask the customer just exactly what they expect in terms of excellent service, ask them how they think you are doing in comparison to those standards, ask them what they like best about doing business with you and what they like least. Ask them what it would take for them to do more business with you and for them to refer you to others. Ask them everything you would like to know. They will tell you!

And don't forget to tell them how much you appreciate their opinions and their advice and their business. Then ask them to come back again!

Day Twenty

Listen

After you have asked, then shut up and listen! Most people think that listening is that time when you are quiet, waiting for your turn to talk. You simply can't afford to do that with your customers. It is the information that the customer has that gives you the ability to meet and exceed their expectations. You have to ask for it, and then listen for it.

The skill of listening is one of the most overlooked customer service skills. Everyone has had courses in talking well and writing well. Several have had additional training in selling and getting along with difficult people and on and on. But few have had a good course in listening. Find one and take it!

Practice active listening. Look at the other person, give good physical feedback by leaning forward and nodding at them. Give good verbal feedback by saying things to them that lets them know you are paying attention. Repeat key words and phrases to them to verify your understanding of what they are telling you.

One of the highest forms of respect to anyone is to listen to their ideas and opinions. You don't have to agree or disagree. Just listen!

Day Twenty-one

Focus on Solutions

Ask for feedback, listen to the feedback. Love your customer and love the customer's problem. All that is important. But it's not enough. While the customer will appreciate all of this and this will make you stand out from the rest of the pack, it's not enough. You have to have solutions. Your customers want solutions. Constantly be looking for solutions to the problems of others. Focus on what it takes to fix things.

Frequently, you can find a solution very quickly by simply asking the customer what it would take to make them happy. Try it. You may be surprised how little it takes to come up with a solution. Other times it will take much longer and require much more effort. Regardless of the route you take, let the customer know that you are a person and an organization that focuses on finding solutions to their problems. Prove to them that you are concerned and want to make them happy by solving problems and not being just another part of the problem.

Day Twenty-two

Communicate

Communicating that we are customer focused involves what we say, how we say it, how we look when we say it, the way we listen, the way our business looks, the way the telephone is answered and more. How are your communications? It doesn't matter what you think, feel or believe if the customer is not having it communicated to them through your actions.

Take a good communications course in order to make sure that what the customer is hearing is what you really want to be saying. As a leader, spend money on your employees to make sure that their communications skills are top quality.

Half the world is composed of people who have something to say and can't, and the other half who have nothing to say and keep on saying it. —Robert Frost

You can have brilliant ideas, but if you can't get them across, your ideas won't get you anywhere. —Lee Iacocca

I will pay more for a man's ability to express himself than for any other quality he might possess. —Charles Schwab

Day Twenty-three

Tell the Truth

Always be honest. There is never a reason to be anything less. If you make a mistake, admit it, apologize and move on! The truth always comes out anyway. Never jeopardize the customer's trust and confidence in you by being deceitful in any way.

Never try to fake it. Customers can see through you and will come to the conclusion that you are insincere in your concern for them and their problems. Avoid using words such as "honestly", "frankly" and "truthfully." Using these words is the best indication that you haven't been that way up until that point.

When you don't know the answer to the customer's question, then tell them you don't know! However, be solution focused and tell them you will be happy to go find out. Then be reliable and find out and let them know the right answer.

Make a decision to be truthful at all costs! You have heard before that "Honesty is the best policy." It is. It is the best customer service policy.

Day Twenty-four

Take Good Notes

One of the best ways to show the customer you really are focused on them is to write down what they tell you. Getting it down in writing has lots of benefits.

First, customers get smarter in direct proportion to the number of notes you take. That's right! They will give you better information and be more to the point when you are writing down what they say.

Secondly, it's a great tool for dealing with irate, difficult, obnoxious customers. Just say, "What you have to say to me is very important and I want to make sure that I get every word of it just the way you are saying it, so I'm going to write it all down." Watch how they will clean it up! They don't want you writing down all of those ugly things they have been saying!

Thirdly, many times you are going to need documentation to refer back to. Memory alone isn't enough. You need a place to go back to prove to yourself and maybe others that you really did everything that you promised to do.

There is simply no substitution for good written documentation. Information is power. Take good notes!

Day Twenty-five

Say Thank You

This is so EASY! Two little words that the customer absolutely loves to hear—thank you! Say thank you because you appreciate them and their business. Say thank you for everything, thank you for coming in, for sharing their time with you, for sharing their problem and for giving you an opportunity to solve it.

In fact, be very thankful when the customer shares their concerns with you. Ninety-four percent of dissatisfied customers simply go away and never come back. If they tell you they are dissatisfied then they are giving you a chance to fix things. Be thankful. And if you do fix things, statistics show that they will be more loyal than ever.

It goes back to the simple principle that good behavior, when rewarded, will be repeated. Reward the customer with your thank you's. Say thank you immediately, say it verbally, say it in writing, be personal and specific. When you reward them in that way, they will come back and keep coming back.

Day Twenty-six

Do What You Say You are Going to Do

Customers come to you to buy the product or service that you sell. Or do they? Aren't they really buying what you say the product or service will do for them? I believe so. Make sure that it does what you say it will do. Make sure you do what you say you will do. If you slip here, then the customer will lose confidence and trust in you and your products and services and will choose to go elsewhere in the future.

This applies to internal customers as well. Employees inside the company may not have the option of choosing who they'll buy their support services from because they only have one department for that service in the company. However, they do have the option of being easy to work with or hard to work with. That's their choice. And because both internal and external customers have a choice, you have to do exactly what you say you are going to do. The product must work the way you said it would. The advertising has to promise benefits that are real. Everything must be the way you said it would be. Everything you say and do must help build trust and establish a better relationship.

Day Twenty-seven

Lagniappe

It is critical for you to do what you say you are going to do. But it's magic when you do more. This will set you apart from the pack. This is the stuff that winners do!

When you consistently meet customer expectations, you'll have a great advantage over competitors who don't. However, the leaders in any industry are the ones who give the customer exactly what they bargained for, exactly what they paid for, exactly what they expected, "and then some." The "and then some" is lagniappe. This is a Cajun word that means you give them everything they paid for and a little bit more; "and then some." For you, it means doing the things that most people won't do. It's writing thank-you notes, calling the customer by name, opening a little early for the person who's standing at your door, delivering a package in spite of the bad weather, being better than you promised, and on and on.

Be creative. Learn what it takes to do what the customer expects. Then surprise them with a little extra. You will probably find that the customer will in turn reward you with a little more of their business than you expected. What a deal!

Day Twenty-eight

Win-Win

This is the goal. Everybody has to win. Whether you are a salesperson, a clerk, a truckdriver, a flight attendant, a computer operator, or the company president, as an individual, you must win. Otherwise, you will soon look for other employment. And the company must win. If the company doesn't win, then it goes out of business and you won't have a job and the service you provide to your customers will go away. Most organizations clearly understand this. They make sure that the company wins and possibly the employees. But when they focus on the customer winning, then they have hit the jackpot!

Because when the customer wins, then it will be the company and the employees that really win. It's really a circle. When the company makes sure that the customer wins, then the customer will make sure that the company wins and in turn, the employee will win.

Never think that any one else has to lose in order for you to win. This is never the case. Make win-win your goal in all situations.

Day Twenty-nine

Five Words for Success

The Customer Is Always Right! This is the only philosophy that will ever allow you to become customer focused. It is an attitude. It is a belief system. And it must be a policy.

The customer can never be wrong. They may be incompetent, ignorant, rude, slow, uncaring, unbearable, and even dishonest. But they are still right. Doesn't seem quite fair, does it? Who promised you fair?

This is hard to deal with sometimes, particularly when you are face-to-face with a customer who is being a total jerk. But it comes down to expectations. We expect our customers to be perfect, and that just isn't going to be the case. Customers are just people, having good days and bad days, and sometimes we get them on one of their bad days. Just remember that it isn't personal. They really aren't mad at you. Some of them are just mad. And they need our understanding and empathy. Not a hard time.

The customer isn't always perfect, but the customer is always right. That's the only thing they can ever be. Just love them the way they are. You need them.

Day Thirty

Make It Personal

In order to become customer focused, you need to adopt these principles personally. Take responsibility for making sure that they are all applied in your day-to-day relationships with customers, both outside and inside your organization. And this has to be regardless of the company's policies and procedures.

You need to have your own personal belief system and attitude that the customer is always right. Personalize your role in assuring win-win. Be positive, proactive, and enthusiastic. The more you become involved in delivering customer focused service the better you will enjoy your job.

If you find your belief in the customer is contradictory to that of your company, then go to another company. Never stay where the customer isn't placed first.

Once you understand and practice all of these principles, you can never compromise. And you'll reap great personal and professional success.

Day Thirty-one

Never Turn Back

Congratulations! You are now on a road with no U-turns; no way of turning back. The rewards you will get from becoming customer focused, satisfying your customers and making yourself and your organization the kind that people want to do business with will keep you encouraged and motivated.

But even if you want to turn back, your customers will never let you. Once you have started delivering great customer service, the customer's level of expectations for you as an individual and for your company will go up. And as you continue the cycle of meeting and exceeding customer expectations, you will find it easier and easier to make those commitments. The personal fulfillment will be unlike anything you have ever experienced before. You won't just have a job, you will have a calling. They won't just be customers, they will be opportunities for you to serve.

The business of life is to move forward. You have started moving forward on a road to great success!

CHAPTER 2

31 Days to Getting Along with Others

Relationships Come In All Shapes & Sizes

There are lots of kinds of relationships. Business relationships; social relationships; church relationships; casual acquaintances; friends; your spouse or significant other; your children; other family members; people you pass on the street, and more.

Relationships will come and go. They will change in intensity and frequency. Some will be good and some bad. Some will last a lifetime and some will only last a moment. That's just the way life is. To expect it to be different is naive.

The key is to understand that every relationship is different, and you have to treat each one differently. You must act and react differently in each relationship. Look for the differences and enjoy them.

The most immutable barrier in nature is between one man's thoughts and another's.
—WILLIAM JAMES

Day Two

People Come in All Shapes & Sizes

People are like relationships; they are all different. That means that you must treat each one differently.

Some people are easy-going and will be a pleasure to know and be around. And some people are the kind that make the hair on the back of your neck stand up every time they open their mouth.

Understand that these differences are normal. Accept people for who they are. Appreciate the differences among individuals that make your relationship with them unique.

When two people always agree, one of them is no longer necessary.   —UNKNOWN

Day Three

Define the Relationship

Defining the relationship is a matter of determining whether the relationship is one between people or one between roles.

Friendship is a relationship between people. Two people choose to be together for simple reasons, such as they like each other.

Other relationships, such as worker-boss, husband-wife, parent-child, businessperson-customer, are relationships between roles. Individuals take on roles like actors take on parts in a play, becoming what they need to be for the good of the overall objective.

When relationships go bad, consider whether it was the people involved or just the roles assumed. Just because roles disagree and are having a problem doesn't mean that the people in those roles must have the same problem.

Defining the relationship will spare you unnecessary blame and hurt.

Day Four

Take Responsibility

Much of what happens in a relationship is beyond your control. You can't help it if the times change, or the players change, or the objectives change. Those things are out of your control.

In fact, the only thing you can control in any relationship, is you. You are the only constant in the relationship factor. So take responsibility for yourself.

Don't count on others to change. Take the lead in confronting the opportunities and the challenges within any relationship. You are the only one you can count on to make things better.

"Out of all the people who will never leave you, you are the only one."
                                    —JOE CHARBONNEAU

Day Five

Be Realistic

Have realistic expectations for your relationships. It would be easier if people were perfect. But they don't always do what we want them to do. They are not always going to care, they may not always understand or give the relationship the amount of time you think it should take. They may not even be as smart as you think they should be.

But this is the big news—you, in all your glory, are not always perfect either! The other person in the relationship is going to have to put up with your good points, as well as your bad points.

We have to realize that relationships are just made up of folks, and folks are just what they are. No more, no less.

Try not to look at your relationships through rose-colored glasses. We are all people, and people are imperfect, just trying to be the best we can.

Day Six

Look In the Mirror

The best place to go to assess the quality of any relationship is to the mirror. Look at yourself and explore what your role is in the relationship, asking:

- How am I carrying out my role?
- How am I acting?
- What should I change to make things better?
- How can I improve the quality of the relationship?
- What additional skills should I obtain?

A personal assessment is important because you are the constant, the person responsible for making the difference in the relationship.

Look at each role you play—father, mother, friend, co-worker, boss, salesperson, etc. Carefully assess where you are, so you can move toward where you need to be.

Relationships are like crucibles, in which our character defects rise to the surface.   —ANONYMOUS

Day Seven

People Change...
But Not Often

People can change. I know that people are able to change because I have seen it many times. But often, we expect more change than we actually get from others. We expect immediate change and sometimes drastic change, and usually this just doesn't happen.

In order to make real progress in any relationship, we need to understand that people are what they are. We must be able to accept them for what they are and meet them where they are. This will prevent you from suffering unnecessary disappointment through unrealistic expectations.

The beginning of life is to let those we love be perfectly themselves, and not to twist them to fit our own image. Otherwise we love only the reflection of ourselves we find in them.

—THOMAS MERTON

Day Eight

Be Prepared

Being prepared means to arm yourself with the knowledge of others, as well as your own good judgment. Psychologists and scientists have conducted extensive research on how to deal with people and build relationships, and many have written books and recorded audio programs on the subject. Reading those books and listening to educational programs can hone your skills in communications, diffuse arguments, deal with difficult people, understand personality differences and much more.

Each of us has relationships that are critical to our personal and professional well being. It would pay us to get all of the skills available through any and all means available to improve the quality of those relationships.

Day Nine

Communications

I believe that all relationship problems can be traced back to communications problems. Successful relationships are based on successful communications. Successful communications happen when two people use all of their communications skills to come to a point of mutual understanding.

Perhaps the real problem is that most of us simply don't understand what communications really is. Communications is not just having the right words to say. It's knowing when to use the right words, how to says those words and knowing the importance of how we look when we say those words. What your momma told you is true, "It's not what you say but how you say it."

Day Ten

Be Proactive

The best way to predict the outcome of any relationship is to take the lead in the relationship. People generally do what is easiest—and it's easier to react or respond to a given stimulus than it is to create one. In other words, give people a behavior to respond to rather than depending on them to determine the appropriate behavior. (Chances are they will choose incorrectly.)

If you lead by being friendly, chances are the other person will respond in kind by being friendly. If I start out mad, then the other person will likely respond in anger. Being proactive puts you in control of the relationship. It's you taking responsibility and setting the pace for the desired outcome.

So assume the attitude you want the other person in the relationship to have. Smile first, say good morning first, tell them you love them first, say that you're glad to see them first. Show them and let them hear you set the tone, the attitude, the mood and the pace for the ideal communication and they will respond in kind.

Day Eleven

Your Attitude

Periodically we all need an attitude check. We need to make sure that we are approaching life and relationships in a positive way. Being positive may not help you do anything better, but it will definitely help you do everything better than being negative will.

Work on making your positive attitude genuine. People can detect a fake. You've seen fakes before. It's when the salesperson realizes you are there and says to themselves, "Oops, there's a customer, time for me to be friendly." In relationships, being a fake is being a flop.

You need to be real all of the time and the only way you should really be is positive. When your attitude is right, looking for and expecting the best from yourself and others and sending positive and loving messages, you will be amazed at the ways others respond.

We must always change, renew, rejuvenate ourselves; otherwise we harden.
                                                        —GOETHE

Day Twelve

Meet People Where They Are

Before any relationship can grow and flourish, we must be able to empathize. To empathize means to seek out and attempt to understand the motives and feelings of another. In order to do this and meet people where they are, you have to be able to put yourself in their shoes. Look at the relationship through their eyes and you will better understand what they need from the relationship.

If you meet people at a different level than where they are at the moment, it becomes extremely difficult to communicate. And if you aren't communicating, then you are at a dead end. Empathizing doesn't mean that you should expect people to deny their feelings. You can't go to a sad person and say, "You shouldn't feel sad, you should be happy!" It's not fair for you to ask someone to deny their feelings of sadness, anger, or even happiness. In order to have the relationship work, then meet them where they are and lead them to where you want them to be.

We don't get to know people when they come to us; we must go to them to find out what they are like. —GOETHE

Day Thirteen

Seek Common Ground

People with common interests naturally relate to each other. The more you are like someone else, or like the same things, then the more willing each of you will be to make the relationship work. That's called having rapport. It is much easier to build a relationship if you share interests and have rapport. And it doesn't really matter if the interest is something very trivial or dramatic.

I travel around the country and meet all kinds of people. I tell people that I'm from Oklahoma, and if they say something like "I've got a sister who lives in Oklahoma," then I can build on that little bit of trivia that we share in common. Or I'll build on the fact that both of us are bald or incredibly handsome. You can do the same thing. Look for ways to establish rapport. Look for common ground: we look alike, think alike, dress alike, have a common experience, or interest or belief.

Day Fourteen

The Best Common Ground

If all else fails in trying to establish common ground then remember the best common ground of all. It's everyone's favorite subject—them. According to Dale Carnegie, author of *How To Win Friends and Influence People*, you can win more friends by showing a genuine interest in other people than you ever can by trying to get other people to show a genuine interest in you.

Being genuinely interested in the other person shows that you have respect for them. If they believe you respect who they are, they will open up, communicate more freely and start to find out interesting things about you. Use the other person as the common ground in starting an effective relationship and they will be interested in having and maintaining a long, successful, mutually beneficial relationship.

Day Fifteen

How Much is Enough?

Relationships are not a 50–50 proposition. 50–50 relationships don't work. What if someone doesn't do their part? Then there is a gap. So how much is enough? 100–100. Relationships only work when both parties are committed to a 100 percent effort. Why? Because few people have the energy to give 100 percent at every moment. When that happens, the other person, who is equally committed to giving 100 percent is there to make up the difference and close the gap.

Of course, there are times when neither party is giving enough to close the gap. But if both parties understand that the commitment is there, then the knowledge that each party has of the other's commitment can fill the gap. Besides, the probability is on your side when both give 100 percent that the gaps will be fewer and farther between.

Day Sixteen

Assessment

Remember the mirror? It's time to go back, now that we've learned new ways to have better relationships.

Make a list of ten relationships and the people in them from all aspects of your life: business, social, civic, family, friends, co-workers, and so on. Look carefully at each of these relationships and ask yourself how you are really doing in each situation. Ask, "Do I look for the common ground?" "Have I shown genuine interest in them?" "How's my attitude?" "Am I being proactive?" "How are my communications skills?" "Do I have empathy and meet people where they are?"

After this assessment you may have new insights into your relationships and a new direction you can take to enhance them.

Few blame themselves until they have exhausted all other possibilities.   —ANONYMOUS

Day Seventeen

Judge not . . .

If the other person in a relationship is different from us we have a tendency to jump to certain conclusions and to become judgmental. And in the process of judging, we start to mentally list all the reasons why we shouldn't like them or care about them or be involved with them.

We need to set all that judgment stuff aside. If we are to have successful relationships, then we need to look for the good in others and not be judgmental about the bad. Search for the common ground, figure out reasons to like the other person and look for any good you can find. Set aside the differences, judge less, condemn less, open your mind and be more accepting.

"Judge not, that you be not judged. For with what judgment you judge, you will be judged; and with the same measure you use, it will be measured back to you."   —MATTHEW 7:1,2

Day Eighteen

Forgive

There are people in your life you need to forgive. Some relationships may be over or some may be suffering from things that happened in the past. In some cases, feelings are hurt so deeply and the damage is so severe, that the relationship may be beyond reasonable repair. Accept that. But you should still forgive and move on in order to build healthy new relationships.

The best place to start the forgiving process is to forgive yourself. Forgive yourself for things you said and did that may have caused hurt to other people. We have all been there and none of us have the ability to change the things we now regret. So forgive yourself and vow to do better next time.

Then forgive other people. If you are ever to be happy, you need to forgive others for who they are and what they have done to you. Call, write, or visit persons in these relationships and express your forgiveness. Most importantly, tell yourself that you forgive these people.

He who can not forgive others breaks the bridge over which he must pass himself.
                                        —GEORGE HERBERT

Day Nineteen

It's Not Personal

When the little lady with the blue hair cuts you off in traffic, she probably didn't mean it personally. When a customer is rude, or if a salesperson is discourteous, they aren't really mad at you personally. They are just responding to your role—as a driver, a clerk or a customer. More than likely, the timing was bad. There we were, the first person available to take it out on. Remember: don't judge. Forgive—and move on. You are responsible.

Nobody is really out to get us as an individual. We sometimes give ourselves too much credit. Generally, people don't know you well enough, don't care that much about you and are really more interested only in themselves at the time. Once we understand that it's just not personal, the actions of others can be taken in stride. We can step back, distance ourselves from the event and move on with little stress to ourselves and the relationship.

When you resent someone they live rent-free in your head.
—UNKNOWN

Day Twenty

Look for the Good

Every single person has good in them. Some do have more than others and some are desperately trying to cover up what little they've got, but it's still there. Look for it. Do an experiment. Look for the good in every single person you see. It may be that they are clean, or have a nice smile, or have shined shoes, or you may have caught them in some small act of kindness. You'll be amazed at how, when you really look for it, you will find good in everyone.

Andrew Carnegie said that we should look for the good in people in the same way we go prospecting for gold. When you go looking for gold, you have to moves literally tons of dirt to find one ounce of gold. But you don't go out looking for the dirt, you go looking for the gold. Do the same with people. Ignore the dirt, and sometimes there is plenty of it, and look for the gold. I promise you that it's there.

The greatest good you can do for another is not just to share your riches, but to reveal to him his own.
—Benjamin Disraeli

Day Twenty-one

Serve

Earl Nightingale said that our rewards in life are in direct proportion to our service. How rewarding are your relationships? How well are you serving?

We need to look for ways to serve other people, ways to do good for them. Serving others is not just a business strategy, it's for all of your relationships: family, social, or with a complete stranger.

The Law of Reciprocity says that the more good we do for others, the more good will be done for us. And if good is done for each person in every relationship, we will all be enriched and our entire world will change. Isn't that exciting?

One thing I know; the only ones among you who will be really happy are those who will have sought and found how to serve.
—ALBERT SCHWEITZER

Day Twenty-two

Give

Generosity is another form of serving. Give freely of your time, talent, gifts, money and stuff to others. And if the giving is unconditional, the reward will be greater than the gift. Each of us has something worthy of giving away. You don't have to have incredible monetary wealth to be a millionaire giver. Give your smile, kind words, a helping hand, or a hug. It may even take more, such as clothes, food and shelter. But the more we give to others, the more likely we are to develop a giving attitude. And a giving attitude forms the cornerstone of a strong relationship.

You give but little when you give of your possessions. It is when you give of yourself that you truly give.   —KAHLIL GIBRAN

Day Twenty-three

Keep Lines of Communications Open

It's important to realize that every relationship has its ups and downs. Things just aren't right, communications fall on deaf ears, roles are out of place, or one of the individuals has grown to a point where the ability or willingness to empathize is gone or is just too difficult. If we are going to be the right kind of person, we may need to give the relationship some freedom. However, backing off of the relationship does not mean backing out.

Without judging, let them know that you still care about them and you still love the person they are. Keep the lines of communications open and give the relationship an opportunity for rediscovery. Sometimes, it's simply a matter of timing. Stay open to the possibility of contact in the future when you both may be able to establish common ground again.

Day Twenty-four

Be Creative

Sometimes relationships become stale and boring. However, I don't really believe that there are boring relationships—just boring people in relationships. Stop being boring! Be more spontaneous! Never be dull! Get out of your rut. Someone once said that a rut is just a grave with both ends kicked out. And a relationship in a rut is dying!

It's up to you. You've already made a commitment to take responsibility and be proactive. So do it! Get creative with your relationship. Look at it differently. Think about your activities. Do you do the same old thing all of the time? Do you always eat at the same restaurants and go to the same place for a vacation or talk about the same things? Then STOP! Surprise each other. Look for unique ways to make the other person in the relationship say "WOW!"

It may be a surprise weekend getaway with your spouse, a ROPES course for your management team, serving the homeless a meal at a community center, or any number of different things. But do something different! The difference makes the difference!

Day Twenty-five

Blame

One of the biggest time-wasters in relationships is trying to determine whose fault it is. We want to know why it happened, how it happened, and who caused it to happen. Somehow we think that if we know those things that we will feel better. Well we won't. It simply doesn't matter who is to blame. It won't change what happened anyway.

The effort you use trying to assign blame should be used in mending the relationship. You give up your power to bring healing to the situation when you put your efforts into determining who is at fault. Besides, making someone else wrong, won't necessarily make you right.

Resentment, criticism, guilt and fear come from blaming others and not taking responsibility for our own experiences.
                                        —LOUISE L. HAY

Life appears to me too short to be spent in nursing animosity or registering wrongs.   —CHARLOTTE BRONTE

Day Twenty-six

Timing

Timing can be a critical element in any relationship. In the best of relationships, the timing has probably been perfect. All conditions are right, the attitudes are in alignment, and all parties are willing to do whatever it takes to make things work. But sometimes the timing isn't right.

We must be sensitive to the issue of appropriate timing at all levels. There is a time to talk and a time to be quiet. There is a time to bring up issues and a time to let them slide. A time to touch and a time not to touch. Timing is key. Wait for the right time. Sometimes the whole relationship must wait for the right time. All things have a season. So do relationships.

Time eases all things.   —SOPHOCLES

Day Twenty-seven

Reality

It is important to understand that as much as we want a good, close relationship, and as hard as we may try—sometimes it just doesn't work. The timing may never be perfect. The other person may just have too many things going on to let us in. Differences may be insurmountable.

The reality is that we must be able to accept this. We can't make everyone happy. And it is unrealistic to think that every relationship is going to be a close, loving, blissful relationship. This kind of expectation will bring you great disappointment. The key is to be open, nonjudgmental and forgiving. Be friendly and loving. Treat people better than they expect to be treated and better than they should be treated. But understand reality. Accept reality.

Reality—what a concept.   —ROBIN WILLIAMS

Day Twenty-eight

Assessment Time Again

One more time. Assess your relationships in terms of the new principles we've learned. Have you kept the lines of communications open? What kind of service are you offering to the people in your relationships? Have you looked for the good in every person? Do you understand that most of the time what happens to you isn't personal? Do you waste time blaming? Are you being creative? Are you being realistic in your expectations?

Constantly check your relationships. This is especially important when things aren't going well. Because the only thing constant is change, you must always be in the process of assessing the various aspects of your relationships.

I believe that every right implies a responsibility; every opportunity an obligation; every possession, a duty.
—JOHN D. ROCKEFELLER

Day Twenty-nine

Move On

In your assessment, you looked at yourself, learned skills, served, committed yourself and accepted that some relationships just won't work. You've done everything we talked about for the last 28 days. Now you need to learn a very important word—NEXT.

If you've honestly done everything you can do, then just say "next" and move on! Find someone else, look for a new customer, search for a new job, find a new set of friends. Accept that some relationships don't and won't work, and move forward. As you move forward through life you will meet new people and find countless opportunities to begin new relationships. The future holds great possibilities. In fact, most of the friends you will have 10 years from now, you don't even know today. So move on to the exciting new relationships that await your discovery.

The business of life is to go forward.   —SAMUEL JOHNSON

Day Thirty

Guilt-free

Beware of guilt! Forward progress can only happen if you move into new relationships guilt-free. Guilt over the past serves no purpose in this universe. You can't go back and fix one thing, you can't re-wind, re-play, re-say, or re-do anything. And to re-live all of the things that went wrong in a relationship simply wastes time and serves no positive purpose. The only thing we can do from past relationships that failed is to learn from them. Learn, assess, and figure out ways to do things differently in the future. Let past relationships be your school for new and better future relationships.

The important thing to remember is that when you have followed all of the principles in this book, you will have forgiven yourself and others. So say "next", start fresh, move on, and go guilt-free into your next opportunity.

Guilt never makes anyone feel better, nor does it change a situation. Stop feeling guilty. Let yourself out of prison.
                                        —Louise L. Hay

Day Thirty-one

Be Receptive

Stay open to relationships. It's necessary to leave all lines of communications open in past relationships for the possibility that they may be reestablished. It is also necessary that we be open to new relationships.

Make yourself the kind of person that others want to come in contact with. Be the friend, spouse, co-worker, boss, employee, and customer you would like to have and indeed you will find that you will have that kind of friend, spouse, co-worker, boss, employee and customer.

Be receptive and open to new people and associations and relationships. Good people are everywhere. The world is overflowing with great folks looking for people just like you. You are the perfect friend for someone. Be receptive to that someone.

CHAPTER 3

31 Days to Getting What You Want

Get a Notebook

Remember how fun it was on the first day of school when you got out your new stack of paper and put it into a brand new 3-ring binder? Clean, fresh, organized and ready for big new things to come that year. You begin getting what you want by doing just that.

Get a 3-ring binder and paper or a spiral notebook because effective today you are going to start getting what you want by writing down what you want.

You can no longer rely on your mind to remember and act upon your saying "Oh, I know what I want." Too many other things can get in the way of your thoughts. You've got to write it down. And you need a notebook that you can organize and categorize with. Break down what you want into three lists of everything you want to be, everything you want to do and everything you want to have. Put together tabs for each of those areas.

Don't attempt to skip this step. You can't skip it.

Work from document, not from thought.   —BRIAN TRACY

Day Two

No Limitations

Start thinking without bounds. Think "NO LIMITS." Remember this question, "What would I attempt if I knew I could not fail?" If you will think in this way, then there are absolutely no limits to what you can accomplish!

Napoleon Hill said, "Whatever the mind can conceive and believe, it can achieve." The operative word in that statement is WHATEVER. You have to drop all thought of lack and limitation. It won't work to say things like, "but I don't have enough money" or "I don't have enough education" or "it's never been done before" or "I'm too fat" or "I'm too old." These are excuses that limit your creativity and your ability to achieve the great things you were meant to achieve. You must get rid of those thoughts and expand your boundaries and think without limits.

Never shoot yourself in the foot before you start the race.

Day Three

What Do You Want to Be?

Now that you're thinking without limits, make a list of everything you want to be. Remember when you were a kid and you talked with your friends about what you wanted to be when you grew up? Do it again right now. Would you like to be more prosperous? Would you like to be an artist, a firefighter, a farmer, or a teacher? What's standing in your way? You can be whatever you want to be. What you are has nothing to do with what you have the possibility of becoming.

Start by opening up your mind to everything you can possibly be. Go to your notebook and write at the top of the page—EVERYTHING I WANT TO BE. Start writing and don't quit until you have at least 25 things in front of you. Sometimes it takes at least 25 items just to get your mind to loosen enough to really get started.

We weren't put here to make a living. We were put here to live our making and by living our making we will make our living.
—LES BROWN

Day Four

What Do You Want to Do?

Think of all the things in your life you would like to do. Remember, no limitations. Don't start saying, "Oh, I'd really like to do that, if only..." There should be no "if only's" in your vocabulary. Dr. Robert Schuller advises that we should change our "if only's" into "move ahead boldly's."

So again go to your notebook and move ahead boldly. Write at the top of the page—EVERYTHING I WANT TO DO. Don't quit until you have at least 25 items on your list. Have you always wanted to scuba dive, meet famous people, travel, watch a baseball game at Wrigley field, or just plant a garden? Then write it down! It doesn't matter how grandiose or how simple. Make a long list of everything in the world you would like to do.

Change your "if only's" into "move ahead boldly's."
—Dr. Robert H. Schuller

Day Five

What Do You Want to Have?

If you are like most people, then you will probably find this one to be the easiest. That's because we all think of what we want in terms of haves. Would you like to have more money? How about a new car, or house, or a new job? This is an easy list and can go on and on, and it should.

The important thing again is to write the list. So go again to your notebook and write at the top of the page—EVERY-THING I WANT TO HAVE. Don't quit until you have at least 25 things. But don't stop at 25 if you feel like going on. And remember—NO LIMITS.

Most people have no idea of what they want, but they are pretty sure they don't have it.

—ALFRED E. NEWMAN

Day Six

How Many Goals?

A lot of people ask "how many goals do I need?" I believe that you need lots of goals, hundreds of goals. The problem is rarely too many goals, it's not having enough goals! And it doesn't matter how farfetched your goals may seem when you are writing them down. Because you are thinking without limits and boundaries, it's easy to have lots of goals.

You have probably heard it said to children, "You want too much." What a lousy thing to say. Or hear! You can never want too much. So write down 100 things you want. And if you can write 100 then you can write 101. And if you can write 101, then you can write 102. Because goals have buddies: companion goals. So write them all down. The idea is to have so many ideas that you have lists of great big goals and lists of little bitty goals. All kinds of goals factor into your everyday life.

It is the achievement of worthwhile goals that will create the future that you want your present to become.

—Larry Winget

Day Seven

Make Them Big

You need some great big goals! Your goals should be so big that they will challenge you to do more, be more and have more than ever before.

If your goal isn't big and motivating and can be reached will little or no effort, then you will never accomplish great things in your life. Some people set goals, but the goal just isn't challenging enough to have them jump out of bed enthusiastically and say, "I've got to get started on this thing NOW!" That's the kind of goal you need!

Set your goal so big that you have to reach for it. There are no unrealistic goals, just unrealistic time frames. And great big goals do take a lot of time, but how much time would have passed if you hadn't been working on your goal? Same amount, right? So think BIG!

Make no little plans; they have no magic to stir men's blood and probably themselves will not be realized. Make big plans; aim high in hope and work, remembering that a noble, logical diagram once recorded will not die.

—Daniel H. Burnham

Day Eight

Make Them Small

How do you eat an elephant? One bite at a time. How do you achieve great big goals? By breaking them down into lots of little bitty goals.

You have to have some very small goals. First, it is easier for you to visualize success when focusing on a small goal. And you need to get in the habit of visualizing success. Then, success with a small goal will give you the courage to go ahead and set and attack big goals. And you will need courage. Achieving small goals will also give you a sense of accomplishment. A feeling that you are a person who gets things done.

So have some small goals on your list. They can be special goals just by themselves or they can be small pieces of big goals.

You eat an elephant one bite at a time.

Day Nine

Make Them Specific

When you set your goals, make them specific. Verrrrrry specific. Most people say, "I want more of this or that." "More" is not specific. Amounts are specific. In my seminars, I ask to see the hands of those who would like to have more money. I get lots of hands. I then ask one of the participants to come to the front of the room. I press a shiny quarter in their hand and congratulate them for achieving their goal. Everyone joins me in a round of applause for this person who has achieved their goal of having more money. But the quarter is not what they had in mind. They had much more than a quarter in mind. But they only stated that they wanted "more." They got more. Twenty-five cents more than they had.

Want to weigh less? How much less, exactly? Want a new house? Where? On what street? How many stories? Brick or frame? With a pool?

Set goals in terms of specifics: minutes, hours, days, weeks, months, years, color, size, dollars, numbers, square feet, etc. Be specific.

You'll never make it as a wandering generality; you have got to become a meaningful specific.   —ZIG ZIGLAR

Day Ten

Make Them Positive

Positive goal setting will put your mind and attitude in the proper place to help you achieve your goals. Negative goal setting focuses on where you don't want to be and on what you don't want to happen. As an example, never say, "I want to quit smoking." Only smokers need to quit smoking. And if you think of yourself as a smoker, then you will act like a smoker. Instead say, "I am a non-smoker." Then you will begin to think and act like a non-smoker. See the difference?

The mind works on the dominant thought. When you tell yourself, "don't eat chocolate," the dominant thought is "eat chocolate." Instead, tell yourself that you only eat healthy foods. The dominant thought is "eat healthy foods" and creates a positive action with a positive result.

So state your goals in a fashion that says what you do want to be, do or have in a positive way. A positive statement that will keep your mind focused on what you want to accomplish and achieve.

Aim at nothing and you'll probably hit it.   —UNKNOWN

Day Eleven

Make Them Present Tense

Most people tend to think about goals in terms of the future. I want or I will or someday. Stop that! From this point on start thinking and writing your goals in the present tense. I am or I have or currently I.

I am a non-smoker. I eat healthy foods. I feel great. I currently weigh (desired weight.) I own (desired thing.) I sell (desired amount.) I earn (desired amount.) See what I mean? Think of yourself as in possession of your desired goals. This will work like a magnet to draw the end result to you.

Avoid the place called "Someday Isle." Someday I'll do this or someday I'll do that or someday I'll have one of those. Putting it into the future fosters doubt and procrastination. Remember that the mind focuses on the dominant thought. Think present tense!

Seize the day! Carpe diem!   —QUINTUS HORATIO FLACCUS

Day Twelve

The Goal Must Be Yours

You can't attack a goal with commitment unless the goal is your goal. You may want to make your boss, or your doctor, or your spouse happy by doing something that they want you to do. But the chances of you accomplishing that goal will be far greater if it's something you want to do.

Goals are personal. The plan to achieve the goal will be personal. No one can write your goals for you. No one can achieve your goals for you.

Go though your list of goals in all the categories of everything you want to be, do and have and verify that the goals are really your very own personal goals. Make sure that your goals reflect your dreams and not those imposed on you by others over the years. When you do something for your reasons, your chances for success multiply dramatically.

Goals must be personal.

Day Thirteen

Your Goals Must Work Together

I love M&M's. At one point in my life I was eating a 2 pound bag every day. I liked it that way. During that same period of time, I had a goal to weigh 165 pounds and have a 34 inch waist. You can't do both. That body and 2 pounds of M&M's a day don't go together. I had a conflict.

Do you have any conflicts? Most people can't play all of the golf they want and still spend enough time with their family. Most people can't eat everything that they want and have the body they want and be as healthy as they want.

Are your goals in conflict? Check them out. Your goals must work together, or one of them won't work.

. . . if one advances confidently in the direction of his dreams and endeavors to live the life which he has imagined, he will meet with success unexpected in common hours.
>   —HENRY DAVID THOREAU

Day Fourteen

Commitment

Become emotionally committed to your goals. In the world of selling we know that people buy emotionally and justify their purchase logically. You will buy into your goals in the very same way. The more emotional you get about anything, the more likely you are to take action on it.

And when you are emotionally committed to the achievement of your goal, you will find ways to make it happen. Become so committed to the accomplishment of your goal that you won't take no for an answer. So committed that nothing less than making it happen will be enough for you. So committed that no one or nothing can talk you out of it or discourage you. Then success is yours!

Logic will not spur you to action and achievement, only emotional commitment will.

Day Fifteen

The Process

All work is a process. And a process is simply a set of steps, that when followed will bring about the desired result. Anything can be accomplished if you follow the right steps in the right order. The key is to follow the steps.

There are no shortcuts. As a child, you probably wanted to be a grown-up. But all the wanting and wishing in the world didn't make it happen. There was no way to short cut physical growth. There is no way to short cut personal growth either. You've got to follow the steps.

So get ready to follow the ten step formula for getting what you want. Don't quit now. You are already farther than 97 percent of the people in the world. You know what you want, you've written it down, you've stated it positively, you know it's your goal and you are committed. So work these next ten steps and actually get what you want!

Even if you are on the right track, you will get run over if you just sit there.
                                                        —WILL ROGERS

Day Sixteen

The Goal

Step One. Pick a goal. Just go to your notebook, to the lists of things you want to be, do or have and select one goal to work through the ten steps. Now write that goal at the top of a brand new sheet of paper.

Be sure that the goal is stated positively and in the present tense. This is very important. Then ask yourself these questions one more time. Is it my goal? Am I emotionally committed to the accomplishment of this goal? Is the goal without conflict in terms of the other things I want to be, do or have? If the answers are yes then you are ready to continue. If the answers are no, then go back to your lists and find a goal that qualifies.

You show me a stock clerk with a goal and I'll show you a person who will make history. But you show me a person without a goal and I'll show you a stock clerk. —J. C. PENNEY

Day Seventeen

Why I Want It

Step two. Why do you really want to be, do or have this thing you have chosen as your goal? In other words, what are the benefits of your achieving this goal?

Go back to your notebook and write Why I Want My Goal at the top of the next page. Then start writing down all of your reasons. Take your time, because you are going to need lots of reasons.

The nice thing about making this list is that it will allow you to learn more about why you want your goal. Will it make you happier? Healthier? More prosperous? Feel better? Live longer?

This list will also be used when things aren't going as well as you had planned for them to go. This is the place you will come when it's time to re-sell yourself on why you wanted to be, do or have this thing in the first place. So do a good job here. You will need this list.

If you have a strong enough why, you can endure any how.
—VIKTOR FRANKL

Day Eighteen

Obstacles

Step three. Identify the obstacles you will encounter along the way. Some might say, "Isn't this negative?" The answer is "NO!" This is realistic. Everything good that you will pursue will have obstacles. That's just the way life is.

Obstacles are also a pretty good indication that you are on the right track. No obstacles—probably not much of a goal. No challenges and no great accomplishment to achieve it. Lots of obstacles—probably a good, challenging, motivating goal that will carry great reward when accomplished.

So go to your notebook and start a list of obstacles. Not excuses. Only legitimate obstacles that you know must be dealt with in order to accomplish your goal.

Good news! An obstacle, when written down, diminishes in power. Somehow, when you write it down it just doesn't seem like as big of a deal as it did before. So write them down so you can prepare a defense.

Obstacles are what you see when you take your eyes off your goals. —Dr. Norman Vincent Peale

Day Nineteen

What I Know

Step four. Go to your notebook again and write at the top of a new page, What I Already Know About How To Achieve My Goal.

The good thing is that you already know something about what it takes to get what you want. So take credit for what you know. Write it down.

You will be amazed at how much knowledge you have accumulated on and about your goal. Especially if it is something you have wanted for a long time. Just make bullet points of key facts and ideas, key sources of information that you have, books you own that contain information about your goal, and any other tidbits of information that might come to mind.

The Lord gave you two ends, one for sitting and one for thinking. Your success depends upon which you use, heads you win; tails you lose.
                                                        —TIM HANSEL

Day Twenty

What I Need to Know

Step five. Information. We all need more information than we have in order to accomplish our goals. We either need to know more about the goal, or more about the process by which to reach the goal, or more about ourselves.

If you desire to weigh less, you may need to know more about nutrition or exercise. If you want to be a better parent, you may need to know about sources of material that are available to help you become one.

The bottom line is that none of us has all of the information that we need in order to become as successful as we deserve to be. Gather information. Determine the resources that are available. Find out what you need to know in order to get what you want.

It's what you learn after you know it all that counts.
—JOHN WOODEN

Day Twenty-one
People Who Can Help Me

Step six. List as many people as you can who will help you achieve your goal. The list may include people you already know, such as your boss, your spouse, your doctor, your minister, priest, or rabbi, a special friend or mentor. Or it may include people you haven't met yet, people you know are experts who could help you achieve your goal.

Back to the notebook and start a new page. List everyone who comes to mind. Caution! When you involve someone in your goals, you are putting yourself on the line. There will be some people who won't be supportive of you. They will tell you all of the reasons you shouldn't, can't, or won't make it. Run from these people. They will not help you achieve your goals. They will keep you from it. And be careful when someone tells you something "for your own good." It rarely does you any good. Remember that this is a list of people who can help you reach your goal, who will encourage you and provide needed information. It is not to include any discouragers or nay-sayers.

Keep away from people who belittle your ambitions. Small people do that, but the really great people make you feel that you too can be great. —MARK TWAIN

Day Twenty-two

The Plan

Step seven. The biggy! You've got to have a plan. Take lots of time and be very careful with your plan. You may want to take more than one page in your notebook for The Plan For Achieving My Goal. Tomorrow when you get out of bed, you are not going to come face-to-face with your goal. But you will come face-to-face with your plan for achieving that goal. The plan is the daily-ness of goal achievement.

Some people will tell you not to worry about this part. They will say to just set the goal and wait for it to come to you and for you to be drawn to it. They are right about that. Goals are magnets. However, the route that they draw you through may not be what you had in mind. You don't want to be dragged kicking and screaming through the ditches and mudholes toward your goal. You want a responsible method of achieving what you want out of life. So never try to side-step the plan. Spend some time on it. Make sure it is workable. Make sure that you can live with it on a daily basis.

The best plan in the world won't work if you won't.

Day Twenty-three

Accomplishment vs. Activity

A lot of folks get so caught up in their plan that they wind up concentrating on the "doing" and not the "getting done." Make sure that your plan focuses on accomplishment and not activity. It never matters what you are doing. It only matters what you are getting done. There is nothing more frustrating than to find out that you are absolutely excellent at doing something that didn't need to be done at all.

If you find yourself getting caught in the activity trap and aren't really moving closer to your goal, then stop! Review the benefits of achieving your goal and make sure that your plan is accomplishment focused. Stop thinking in terms of "to-do" lists and start thinking in terms of "to-get-done" lists. End each day by asking yourself how much closer you moved toward your goal that day. Understand that everything you do either moves you closer to your goal or farther away from your goal. Then only do things that move you closer to your goal. Say no to everything else. Become accomplishment focused.

It's not what you do, it's what you get done!   —Larry Winget

Day Twenty-four

Get Started

You are ready! You've defined the goal, you know what information you have and need, you have identified who can help you and you have written an accomplishment-focused plan. Now it is time to really get started. It's time for action. Action changes results and will get you what you want.

Some people stall right here because they are afraid to get started. They believe that starting puts them at risk of failing. Let's get this point straight. If you get started you have already won! Failure never comes from doing, only from not doing. Even if you don't do it as well as you wanted to do it, or as well as you could do it or as well as you will do it next time, the point is YOU DID IT! You are a success!

The way to do things is to begin.　　　　—HORACE GREELEY

He who hesitates is last.　　　　　　　　—MAE WEST

Don't talk about it—do it!　　　　　　　GRANT G. GARD

If you don't know how to do something—START!
　　　　　　　　　　　　　　—THE SELF STARTER'S CREDO

Day Twenty-five

Today!

Step eight. What will I do today? You must begin today. Not tomorrow. Not next week. Now!

There is a Chinese proverb that says the journey of a thousand miles begins with a single step. Take your first step today. It doesn't have to be some giant leap for mankind. All it takes is a baby step. Some small amount of forward progress toward getting what you want.

Go to your notebook and write out what you are going to do today. Maybe it's just pick up the phone to call one of those people who can help you. Or maybe it's going to the bookstore to buy a book with the information you need. However small it may seem, it is moving you closer to where you want to be and that's one step closer than you have ever been before!

If you are going to change your life, you need to start immediately and you need to do it flamboyantly.

—WILLIAM JAMES

Day Twenty-six

Set a Completion Date

Step nine. Set a date for achieving your goal. Go to your notebook again and write that targeted completion date down.

Some goals are life-long goals and don't really have dates to be finished. Things like being a better spouse or parent, or to be healthier. But you still need check-up dates to determine your progress and to make sure that you are staying on target.

Other goals will have definite dates for achievement and completion. For these goals it is important to stay extremely focused on the accomplishment within the time frames you have set. However, sometimes you will reach the date before you reach the goal. When that happens, review your plan. Re-sell yourself on why you wanted this thing in the first place. Get emotionally committed all over again and restart! Don't give up, just get after it again!

There will also be times when you will reach the goal before you reach the completion date. When that happens— CELEBRATE!

Day Twenty-seven

Celebrate!

Step ten. Celebrate. Every successful venture needs to be rewarded. And you have just achieved a personal success, you have achieved your goal. So set a reward and celebrate—you deserve it!

Go to your notebook and write down How I Am Going To Celebrate. Make it good. The bigger the accomplishment the bigger the celebration. Please don't skip this step. You need to recognize, reward and celebrate your victories! The celebration can be huge or simple, a party or a prayer, a banquet or a sunrise. But do it!

A word of caution regarding rewards and celebrations. The celebration should never be in conflict with the goal. If you are celebrating weight loss, then don't reward yourself with a pie. If you've stopped smoking, then don't celebrate with a cigarette. See what I mean?

Decide in advance what the celebration will be. Sometimes the extra incentive will keep you on track to help you achieve your goal and get what you want.

Day Twenty-eight

Life Areas

Do one more thing. Look at your goals to make sure you are setting goals in all the different areas of your life. Your life has seven areas:

- Mental / Continuing Education
- Physical / Health
- Spiritual
- Career / Business
- Social / Civic
- Financial
- Family

Go back to your How To Get What I Want notebook and make a separate page for each of these seven life areas. Write down specific goals to achieve in each area. Look back at what you have already written and begin splitting your goals into these areas. Just by becoming aware of these areas you will be stimulated to think of new goals that you hadn't thought of before. Write them down.

Success is being all you can be in each area of your life without sacrificing your ability to be all you can be in each and every other area of your life.   LARRY H. WINGET

Day Twenty-nine

Balance

As you consider the various areas of your life, check your goals for balance. Without balance, I question your ability to be truly successful, and I know you will find it impossible to be truly happy.

Balance is critical because none of us is one dimensional. We all have the seven life areas. And each area deserves and demands attention. So check your goals to see if you are giving your best and have a plan for becoming your best in every area.

You may find that you have listed goals in only one area. That indicates a lack of balance and the other areas will suffer. Of course, temporary imbalance is normal. When you start any effort in one area, the others will suffer slightly. So be aware of this and be cautious so as not to become permanently out of balance.

The most important word in the English language is balance.
—Tom Hopkins

Day Thirty

Reality Slumps

There will be high points and low points in going after what you want. Life is just that way. Everything good will be challenged and you will be faced with problems and set-backs. Sometimes you will just get tired. This is all normal and to be expected.

So don't be naive and expect it all to come to you like magic. It won't. If it were a snap to get the big things out of life then everyone would have them. And you don't have to spend much time looking around to see that's just not the case. You are one of a few people who has made the decision to step away from the pack and get what you really want. That means that you are going to be faced with situations most people just never have to face. Be courageous. Know that slumps happen from time to time and that it's normal. Then move on!

Many of life's failures are men who did not realize how close they were to success when they gave up.   —THOMAS EDISON

Day Thirty-one

Do It Again

Congratulations! You have set a goal and followed all ten steps through to completion. The key to long term success, happiness, achievement and prosperity is to do it again. You did it once and lived, so I know you can do it again.

Go back to your How To Get What I Want notebook and pick another goal and follow the ten steps again and get something else that you want.

If fact, out of the hundreds of goals you probably have listed by now, pick four or five in various life areas and start on those. Be sure to write out the ten steps for each and follow the process exactly as you have learned.

When you have done this a few times, you will have formed a habit. A habit of goal achievement. A habit that will allow you to get everything in life you want. Everything in life you deserve!

CHAPTER 4

31 Days to Leadership

Definitions of Leadership

To begin, we need to look at just a few of the many definitions of leadership.

A person who leads others along a way; a guide.
—AMERICAN HERITAGE DICTIONARY

The aim of leadership should be to help people and equipment and gadgets to do a better job. —DR. DEMING

The goal of most leaders is to make people think highly of the leader, but the goal of the outstanding leader is to make people think highly of themselves. —UNKNOWN

Leadership is inspiring confidence in others.
—GENERAL GEORGE S. PATTON

The task of the leader is to get his people from where they are to where they have not been. —HENRY KISSINGER

Leadership is the ability to decide what is to be done and then to get others to want to do it. —DWIGHT D. EINSENHOWER

Day Two

Take Responsibility

You are responsible. You are responsible for your own style of leadership. You are responsible for your team. You are responsible for results: for the results you and your team have achieved up until now and responsible for the results they will achieve in the future.

You must take responsibility. It doesn't do any good to point the finger of blame elsewhere, because it's up to you. You can't blame circumstances. Things like the economy and your geographic area just don't matter. You can't blame your employees. You can't even blame the company or any policy or procedure. You can't blame anything or anyone. That is, if you are going to be a successful leader. Leaders take responsibility.

Responsibility is where it starts and where it ends. You are responsible.

There are no bad soldiers, only bad officers.

—NAPOLEON

Day Three

Accept Accountability

Accountability is somewhat different than responsibility. Accountability goes beyond responsibility and says that you are not only responsible for your team and its results, but you are willing to be held accountable. Are you willing?

This is a tough one. There are many leaders and managers with the title and the responsibility who are ineffective in the workplace because they aren't willing to be held accountable. If you are that way, then get out now. Be willing to be accountable. Be proud to stand for who and what you represent.

This means that if it all goes wrong, they will come to you and you will stand tall and take it—willingly.

Credentials are not the same as accomplishments.

—Robert Half

Day Four

Assessment Time

How are you doing? What kind of a leader are you? Do you often point the finger of blame elsewhere? Do you shirk responsibility when things get tough? Are you proud enough of the results of you and your team to be held accountable? All are tough questions that must be answered. You have to take some time to evaluate your skills and your style and your willingness.

Ask for input from a trusted colleague. Ask for input from your subordinates. Ask for input from your boss. Have them tell you what they think a good leader must be and do. Then have them tell you what your strong and weak points are against their definition. Use this information to write out an assessment of your current leadership abilities. This will provide the basis for your improvement.

If he has the qualities of a boss, he will thrive; if he doesn't, no matter what he does or says, he is not going to thrive.
—MILTON GLASS, GILLETTE

Day Five

Study Time

You've done your assessment and now it's time to go to work on yourself. School is never out for any of us, but especially for those who lead others. Let me make a few recommendations of books for you to read.

13 Fatal Errors Managers Make And How You Can Avoid Them: W. Steven Brown

On Becoming A Leader: Warren Bennis

The Greatest Management Principle In The World: Michael LeBoeuf

Top Performance: Zig Ziglar

Bringing Out The Best In People: Alan Loy McGinnis

Getting The Best Out Of Yourself And Others: Buck Rodgers

Leadership Secrets of Attila The Hun: Wess Roberts

Leadership Is An Art: Max DePree

Day Six

The Physical Environment

The physical space that you and your team occupy can effect your results. Sloppy environment = sloppy results.

Your office should be a monument to your success. Make it look as good as you can afford for it to look. Nothing extravagant is necessary unless you can truly afford it. I have made dumps look good with fresh paint and a few nice pictures. People perform better when they feel good about their surroundings.

Keep your desk and office clean. It is impossible for you to tell your group to get organized when you can't see the top of your desk. "But that's how I work best!" Wrong! Everyone works better with an organized system of paperwork and projects. Clean off your desk and clean up your office. Set an example for others to follow. Then insist on it. You don't have to be a neat freak, but insist on organization.

You don't need paper shuffling to be successful.
—JOE GRIFFITH

Day Seven

The Atmosphere

Look around you. What kind of atmosphere does your office have? Your office does have an atmosphere; a feeling that will determine how people perform. Are people excited, bored, scared, quiet, serious, fun-loving? The atmosphere within your office area will have an impact on all who enter, especially customers. And the atmosphere within your area is your responsibility.

Create an atmosphere of enthusiasm and positiveness where people enjoy what they do.

An atmosphere where mediocrity will be not be accepted and where people accept only the best from themselves and each other.

An atmosphere that this is a place where things get done.

Create an atmosphere that this is a sacred place where everyone only speaks well of each other and of the customer.

—LARRY H. WINGET

Day Eight

You Set the Pace

You set the pace. You are the leader. Others will follow your example. Others will follow your lead.

If you show up late, then you have sent the signal that it's not important to be on time. If you abuse the company expense account, then you are saying that it's okay to steal from the company. If you talk bad about customers, then you can bet your employees will. If you talk bad about other departments, they will too. If you talk bad about your boss, then it's obviously fine for them to talk bad about you.

Your people will use you as an example for their behavior and their attitude. So set a good example. Speak well of others, especially the customer. Have great work habits. Be positive and enthusiastic. Be the kind of employee you want to have.

The speed of the leader is the speed of the pack.
—A SAYING IN THE YUKON

Day Nine

The Right Group of People

This is the biggest challenge: putting together the right group of people. If you are starting fresh you have a better chance, but sometimes you just have to work with what you've got.

Remember this about people:

Attitude is more important than skill. Technical skills and abilities can be trained.

Some people have the words of a winner and the actions of a loser. They are losers. Regardless of what they say and how they say it. They are known as "articulate incompetents." Beware!

The best predictor of future behavior is past behavior.

People are a firm's most important asset. If you have an excellent product but only mediocre people, the results will be only mediocre. —RICHARD S. SLOMA

Day Ten

Expectations

Most problems in business could be solved prior to their happening if we would just lay out expectations clearly in advance.

People want two things from any relationship. First, they want to know what is expected from them. Second, they want to know what they can expect from you.

Most problems come when expectations are undefined, not explained clearly in advance and given no time frames. They also come when we do not communicate expectations effectively.

Nine-tenths of the serious controversies which arise in life result from misunderstanding.   —Louis D. Brandeis

Day Eleven

Ways to Communicate Expectations

Here are just a few of the many ways you can communicate expectations.

Job Descriptions are the best way to communicate what you want from an employee. However, they are usually covered only when the employee is hired and perhaps in reviews or when the employee has committed some infraction.

Periodic Reviews can also be excellent ways to update and give feedback on expectations. They can be on a regular basis, or they can be more spontaneous, even on a project basis.

Group meetings are also a good way to cover expectations. But be careful here. Meetings are normally too frequent, poorly planned and poorly executed.

If people around you will not hear you, fall down before them and beg their forgiveness, for in truth you are to blame.
—FYODOR DOSTOYEVSKY

Day Twelve

Time Frames

Start communicating in terms of when you want things to happen. A leader frequently communicates what needs to happen, but leaves off the time frame that puts the project into a perspective of accomplishment. So, it's left up to the employee to interpret whether it is a "wouldn't it be nice to get this done" or a "this ought to be done" or "I have to get this done!"

If the time frame is not clearly stated, the type of leadership style will imply a time frame. For example, if you have a very powerful leadership style, the employee automatically thinks your request is a "have to get done" when it was really only a "wouldn't it be nice to get this done." A moderate leadership style can imply an "I would appreciate you doing this when you get around to it" when it was actually an "I really need this ASAP!"

Don't expect people to read your mind. Communicate your time frame for accomplishment clearly in advance. That way no one will be disappointed.

Day Thirteen

Communicate

When someone says, "communicate" the first thought is simply one-on-one verbal conversations either in person or on the telephone. But it can also mean talking to groups of people in meetings or even to a huge audience. It can also mean communicating in writing through letters, memos, newsletters, evaluations and proposals.

Whether you are teleconferencing, speaking to a crowd or leaving a note for your spouse, the important thing to remember is to make it clear. Don't expect anyone else to read your mind, or understand your buzzwords or colloquialisms. Make sure you are communicating your ideas succinctly and in a way the other person or group can understand.

I will pay more for a man's ability to express himself than for any other quality he might possess. —CHARLES SCHWAB

By definition, communication means two-way communication. Insecure individuals don't like it. Bosses don't like it, but leaders and innovators do like it.
—MARK SHEPHERD, TEXAS INSTRUMENTS

Day Fourteen

Be Able to Communicate

You communicate in these ways: through content, or what you have to say; through verbal skills, or how you say what you have to say; and non-verbally, or how you look when you say what you have to say. Studies conclude that our effectiveness in communicating with others is based on these proportions: content is 7 percent; verbal skills are 38 percent; and non-verbal skills are 55 percent. Surprised? It's a heck of a thing to find out at this point in your life that what you have to say is just not that important—only 7 percent!

To be an effective leader, you must learn how to improve your effectiveness in each of these areas of communications. There are many good sources to learn these skills. Try Toastmasters, Dale Carnegie or contact your state chapter of the National Speakers Association for training they might offer. I also recommend the book, *How To Get Your Point Across in 30 Seconds Or Less*, by Milo Frank.

You can have brilliant ideas, but if you can't get them across, your ideas won't get you anywhere.   —LEE IACOCCA

Half the world is composed of people who have something to say and can't, and the other half who have nothing to say and keep on saying it.   —ROBERT FROST

Day Fifteen

Listen!

Listening is probably the most overlooked leadership skill and communications skill. Leaders normally have the attitude that it is what they know that is the most important thing. To be a great leader, it is important to understand that it is the information that others have that is the most important thing.

Employees have information that will tell us how to motivate, stimulate and inspire them to action.

Customers have information that will tell us the direction our decisions should take us to meet and exceed their expectations.

The only way to get this information is to ask good questions and then listen intently to the feedback we receive.

One of the best ways to persuade others is with your ears—by listening to them. —DEAN RUSK

Big people monopolize the listening. Small people monopolize the talking. —DAVID SCHWARTZ

Day Sixteen

Get Out There With 'em!

Tom Peters, author of *Thriving On Chaos*, says it all. Get your MBWA. Management By Walking Around. You've got to get out there among the troops. You don't have to know how to do their job, but you do have to know what it takes for them to do their job. You have to show a genuine interest in their job and in them.

Be willing to get out there by their side, ask good questions about their job and then listen. Be with them as they answer the telephones, as they handle customer complaints, as they deliver customer service, as they are selling, hanging wire on a pole, packing cases and more! Whatever job it is you are supervising or leading, you must know what the job entails. You have to be able to empathize with your people. Meet them where they are—where they work!

A leader is like a battalion commander who isn't content to read the menus but insists on going into the mess hall to taste the food himself. Not only does he know more about what's being fed to his subordinates, but he's considered a better leader by his troops.   —PETER DRUCKER

Day Seventeen

People are Different

Every person is unique. You have to understand that Employee A cannot be managed in the same way as Employee B. Being sensitive to the uniqueness in every person will help you communicate more effectively and get more done through each employee.

Many people have enough similar characteristics that they can be grouped into certain categories. Companies have developed testing programs to help you better understand the various types of people you employ. Some may have higher energy levels than others; they may respond to different stimuli; some are more visual while others are audio or kinesthetic. The more you learn about the different styles of people and understand how to approach individuals as individuals, the better your results will be.

Celebrate the differences in people. When two people are exactly alike, you have one too many. —LARRY H. WINGET

Day Eighteen

Be Flexible

A good leader is flexible in dealing with people. Since everybody is unique, each person has to be led a little differently. This means you cannot use only one leadership style with every employee if you want to achieve optimum results. For some it will work, but for others it will only serve to alienate and demotivate them.

You have to meet people where they are in order to lead them where you want them to go. Empathize with their specific needs, goals and desires, and learn what it takes to create an atmosphere where each person is highly motivated. You have to listen, get involved and communicate effectively. Then create an action plan just for that person, involving the employee in setting performance goals and even the rewards that mean the most to that individual.

There are times when even the best manager is like the little boy with the big dog waiting to see where the dog wants to go so he can take him there.   —LEE IACOCCA

You've got to throw different pitches to different batters.
          —DON HUTSON

Day Nineteen

Educate

Educate your people! Provide them with training. Training that will improve their ability to perform and to carry out their assigned tasks. Too many leaders have the assumption that everyone knows what it takes to do the job. That is an unfair assumption. Especially if they have been hired from another organization. Just because they have been a Customer Service Representative for XYZ Company doesn't mean that they know how to be a Customer Service Representative for your company. Titles mean different things to different people and companies. So provide training in how you want it to be done. Never assume that they already know.

Provide training in life skills. It is important to have people who know how to set and achieve goals, make decisions, manage their time, communicate, listen, get along with others, and have a good attitude. These are more important than any technical skills they might have. Mediocre leaders train their people to be better employees. Outstanding leaders train their employees to be better people.

To improve a company fast, develop people fast.
—ANDRALL E. PEARSON

Education is an investment—and never an expense.
—NICK GOBLE

Day Twenty

Rewards and Recognition

Michael LeBoeuf said in his powerful book, *GMP: The Greatest Management Principle In The World*, that what gets rewarded gets done. When your employees accomplish what is expected you must recognize and reward their efforts if you want to continue getting the type of performance you have received.

Recent studies indicate that the number one thing people want from their job is recognition of a job well done. Not money. To be a successful leader, you need to celebrate and reward the achievements of your subordinates. This is not just because you want the behavior repeated, but also because you want to become involved in appreciating their accomplishments. Everyone wants to know that they are appreciated. This can be as simple as a little note passed to the employee, to announcements in meetings, to newsletter articles, plaques, books and educational audio programs. The important thing to remember is to acknowledge their contribution. Your approval is highly desired by your people and will be motivating. You will also be rewarded in turn with continued outstanding performance.

When the number of awards is high, it makes the perceived possibility of winning high as well. And then the average man will stretch to achieve.
—THOMAS J. PETERS AND ROBERT H. WATERMAN

Day Twenty-one

Guidelines for Rewarding People

There are five basic guidelines for rewarding people:

Do it immediately. This creates a great impression on the person receiving the praise. Plus it encourages them to repeat the performance more quickly, which benefits everyone.

Make the reward specific. Things like, "you're doing a great job" are just too general. A compliment like, "I really like how you handled that customer" will work much better.

Praise publicly as well as privately. People want and need recognition in front of their peers. It will also set an example for others to follow.

Be creative. Send an "I appreciate you because . . ." note or telegram or hold a surprise party. Traditional letters and plaques are fine, but the unusual will be remembered.

Keep rewards positive. "Why can't you always do this good?" is not a reward, it is a reprimand. Make sure you reward positively, recognizing the good.

Day Twenty-two

Say Thank-you

"Please" and "Thank you" were ingrained into us in child-hood as simple courtesies. And yet, "thank you" is an extremely overlooked form of reward and recognition by many managers and leaders. Many think "why should I thank them, that's what they get paid to do." Yes, people get paid to do their job. But if you want above standard performance, then some recognition is in order.

This is the easiest reward you can offer as a leader. Just verbally say thank you to your employees. And be very, very specific. The more specific you are, the more meaningful the thank you will be.

Say it often—make it specific—say it in person—say it in writing. But no matter how you say it, SAY IT!

So is a word better than a gift.
                    —BIBLE: APOCRYPHA, ECCLESIASTICUS 18:16

If you want employees to improve, let them overhear the nice things you say about them to others.   —HAIM GINOTT

Day Twenty-three

Write It Down

Recognize a job well done in writing. While it is important to say thank you in person and recognize people in public, writing it down will somehow make it more permanent. Written thank you's and rewards also tend to grow in the mind of the person. They can refer back to the written documentation often and recall how they felt when they first got the letter, certificate of appreciation, plaque, or hand-written note.

One of the most powerful forms of recognizing employees in writing is the simple "I appreciate you because . . ." referred to earlier. This is a simple slip of paper, not too big, that says "I appreciate _____, because _____. Have them pre-printed and use them to reward small but specific accomplishments by your people. You will be amazed at how these will impact overall performance. People will tend to keep these little slips in order to improve their self confidence and build their own self esteem. Have an "I Appreciate _____ Day" and ask that everyone contribute an "I appreciate" to a certain person. Pass around the privilege of being appreciated. Give everyone the opportunity to get written positive feedback on their performance.

Day Twenty-four

Results!

Like it or not, you always get results. Results are everything. When it's all said and done, people don't ask "How?" they ask "How many?" You've set expectations for what you want from your employees. You and your employees have set and attacked specific goals. Goals that are achieved are called results. This is what it's all about. Achieving desired results quickly, profitably, and accurately.

Be sure to set your goals and objectives in ways that can be measured—how many sales you want to close, how many new clients you want, what amount of profit you desire, how many hours should be invested, or what productivity levels you need to achieve. Then measure to see if you accomplished what you set out to do. Track your progress. Find out what is being done.

Focus on accomplishment—not activity. What you do is of little or no consequence. What you get done is everything!

It is possible to spend your time working efficiently on unimportant problems which, even if solved, will bring no glory to you and no profit to the company.
—ROBERT H. HENRY, HUMORIST

Day Twenty-five

Participate

If both the janitor and the company president failed to show up for work for two weeks, at the end of the two weeks, who has been missed the most? The janitor! That's because, in most cases, the janitor is more involved in the day-to-day operations than the president.

Staying in the corner office with the plans and the numbers goes against every principle of a good leader. You can't communicate, listen, set realistic expectations or get good results if you don't participate in the action.

A participative leadership style doesn't mean that you have to give up your role or authority. It simply means that you get involved with the people doing the work, learn what it takes to get it done, and empower employees to take responsibility. The result is creative employees who will go the extra mile because they know you care!

People who are going to be good managers need to have practical understanding of the crafts in their business.
                    —PHILIP OXLEY, PRESIDENT, TENNECO

Day Twenty-six

Delegate

You've heard it before, "If you want it done right, then do it yourself." This is impossible for a busy leader to do. There is simply too much to do to do it all yourself. So you must learn when to delegate.

It can be hard for leaders to delegate because they probably have the experience, skills and talent to actually do the job themselves. They think that to delegate would mean to abdicate responsibility and maybe sacrifice quality.

Others don't like to delegate because someone else might do it better than they could do it and this would diminish their authority or control. This is the sign of an insecure leader. Good leaders hire people smarter than they are or train people to do a better job than they can do. This proves that the leader is indeed the smartest of all.

When you do for a man what he can and should do for himself, you do him a great disservice.   —BENJAMIN FRANKLIN

Proper delegation is an indication of a manager's trust and faith in his people.   —JAMES F. EVERED

Day Twenty-seven

Rules for Delegation

How do you know when you need to delegate? Here are four simple questions:

Can it be done faster by someone else?

Can it be done better by someone else?

Can it be done by someone who likes doing it more than I do?

Can it be done cheaper by someone else?

If the answer is yes to any of these questions, than by all means let someone else do it!

Bonus rule: When at all possible, only do what you uniquely were hired to do. You were hired because you had something special to bring to your job. Do that special thing and let others do theirs.

Don't do anything someone else can do for you.
                                    —BILL MARRIOTT, SR.

Day Twenty-eight

Step Back

Now you need to step back and allow people to do their own work. You've educated them and given them the skills, you've worked with them to set expectations, encouraged them and recognized and rewarded their accomplishments. They have proved that they can do it. So step back and get out of their way!

There are many benefits to stepping back. One, you are showing confidence in your people and trust that they really can do it by themselves. Two, you get the time to regroup and rejuvenate yourself. Everyone needs time to get better and to relax. You, as the leader, need this more than anyone. Take these few precious moments and educate yourself by listening to an educational, motivational audio program. Or watch some of the great video tapes that are available on leading and managing others. Learn to meditate and take mini-vacations in your mind to reduce stress. Take an hour off and go play. Take a walk. Learn how to step back in order to avoid burnout.

Where freedom of play has been lost, the world turns into a desert.
　　　　　　　　　　　　　　　　　—JURGEN MOLTMANN

Day Twenty-nine

Your Right

As a leader you have certain rights. You always have the right to evaluate the performance of a subordinate. Always. This is one of the things you are paid to do.

There are also some areas where you have no rights. While you always have the right to evaluate performance, you never have the right to evaluate the performer. Some leaders overstep their boundaries and attack individuals. That's just not fair. Your role is to get things done through the actions of other people. Evaluate their actions, their performance, and their results.

The person who has been punished is not thereby simply less inclined to behave in a given way; at best, he learns how to avoid punishment. —B. F. SKINNER

Criticism should be like a sandwich. If you want to motivate people, slip the criticism in between layers of praise. —HENRY C. ROGERS

Do not forget little kindnesses and do not remember small faults. —CHINESE PROVERB

Day Thirty

Mediocrity

Never tolerate mediocrity. Mediocrity is your worst enemy. If you tolerate mediocrity in one employee it has a negative impact on all employees. The good employees will say, "Look, they are getting by with it, so I don't have to do as good a job as I have been doing." Then your best performers will start giving you mediocre behavior. And tolerating mediocrity will also allow your worst performers to say, "Why should I improve, they let me get by with it the way it is."

Mediocrity makes everyone a loser. The customer loses by not getting the best of the employee or company. The company loses by wasting money on mediocre performance. The good performer loses by watching a mediocre performer get by with it and developing like behavior. Mediocre performers lose because they aren't doing their best and know that they are stealing from the company. And the leader loses because he or she will lose the respect of the good employees, the mediocre employees, the customer and the company.

Set and demand standards of excellence. Anybody who accepts mediocrity—in school, in job, in life—is a guy who compromises. And when the leader compromises, the whole organization compromises. —CHARLES KNIGHT EMERSON

Day Thirty-one

Good Leaders Know When to Say Good-bye!

There comes a time when the leader must cut people loose and send them on to a career enlargement opportunity. Some people simply must be de-hired.

Tolerating mediocrity or poor performance does no one any good. People must have the ability to do the job or the desire to do the job. If neither exist, then find them a new job. A job within the company where their desire and ability matches the requirements or give them the freedom to pursue another job with another company where they can find a match.

Good leaders must be able to say good-bye. While it can be difficult, it is still a necessary part of leadership.

It isn't the people you fire who will make your life miserable, it's the people you don't fire.   —HARVEY MACKAY

Managers often avoid firing because it's unpleasant. But getting rid of the bad performers is as good a tonic for the company as a reward can be for a star performer.

—ARTHUR BOLDGER

CHAPTER 5

31 Days to Making More Sales

Talk to More People

That's the number one key to making more sales! You see, it doesn't matter how good you are, if you will talk to more people, then you will close more sales. If you are talking to ten people per day, try talking to eleven. That's 220 more people per year. If you close one out of every ten, then that's over 20 more sales every year! What would that do for your income?

So figure out a way to talk to more people. Call more people on the telephone. See more people in person. Try group prospecting. Work faster. Come in earlier. Stay later. Skip your breaks and shorten your lunch hour. Anyone and everyone can make more sales simply by talking to more people.

The more people you talk with, the more sales you will make!

Day Two

Give Away Ten Business Cards Per Day

This sounds easy doesn't it? It is. Even if you don't see ten qualified prospects every day you can still give out ten business cards every day. Give them to the person at your dry cleaners, the restaurant, to your mail carrier, the sales clerk at the retail store; EVERYWHERE. Get your cards in circulation!

You will be amazed at how business cards travel around. There are countless stories of huge sales that have been closed all as a result of a business card traveling through the hands of a number of people and finally ending up in just the right hand at just the right time.

Bonus! Collect business cards from everyone you meet. It will make them feel important and will help you build a strong base of contacts for a mailing list.

Day Three

Smile

It's the first thing people notice about you. And it's almost like magic. Greet someone with a smile and they will almost always return it to you. Smiling makes customers feel better about themselves and about you. A smile will diffuse an uncomfortable situation or calm an irate customer. It is a universal symbol that is understood by all, regardless of their language, age or beliefs.

None of us smile as much or as big as we think we do. So smile bigger and more often than you think you need to. Ask a friend to judge your smile. See if they can tell when you are smiling. A smile is your best sales tool. Learn to use it.

"Sometimes a smile is the only weapon you have."
—ROGER RABBIT

Day Four

Have a Terrific Handshake

This is the first, last and probably only physical contact you will have with your customer. It is your first non-verbal sales approach. Make it a good one. Nothing is worse than grabbing someone's hand and getting the feeling that you need to wash your hands because you've just touched something dead.

Make your handshake firm without being vice-like. Friendly without being mushy. Confident without being pushy. Always look the person square in the eye when you are shaking their hand. Never pump the hand or grab the fingertips. Never hold on too long. And NEVER discriminate between the sexes when shaking hands. The rules are EXACTLY the same for all people in business. EVERY TIME!

If you want above average sales results, then get an above average handshake.

Day Five

Be Really Nice

Did you ever give your money to someone who wasn't nice to you? Probably. But I'll bet you didn't do it more than once, at least not by choice. So be nice to people. Everyone likes to do business with nice people. That means to smile, be friendly, be concerned about their needs and empathetic toward their problems.

And be nice all of the time. Not just when it's convenient, or when they are being nice to you or when you feel like it. But all of the time!

Remember what your Momma told you, "Be nice!"

All of the money you are ever going to have is currently in the hands of someone else. Be nice to them!

Day Six

Learn How to Introduce Yourself

Your introduction is critical. You have to be able to introduce yourself and tell what you do with enthusiasm and without hesitation. You must also be succinct. Thirty seconds is more than enough time to explain who you are and what you do. Any longer than that and you have become a bore.

And when you introduce yourself, don't hesitate to say that you are a sales professional. Never apologize for being a salesperson. Sales keep our country alive and sales is the highest paying profession on earth.

Record yourself. Fine-tune what you say and how you say it. Make it powerful.

Sell yourself through your introduction.

Day Seven

Master the First Two Minutes

Introductions are over. Now you have two minutes to get their attention and create interest in your product and in you. If you lose them here, it's going to be uphill the rest of the way. So get everything working for you: your smile, your handshake, your introduction.

Then know the first two minutes of your presentation so well that if I called you at 3:00 AM you could give it to me enthusiastically and without hesitation. Have it include an absolutely knock-your-socks-off benefit statement. Make it personal. Make it as specific as possible to them, their business or their industry. Practice it. Rework it and try it out until it works. Then go beyond memorization and make it a part of you.

Be as good as you can as quick as you can.

Day Eight

Ask for Referrals

The easiest prospect to sell is one you have been referred to. When a friend, relative, business associate or satisfied customer says to someone, "You should meet Larry" or "You should see what he's done for us," then the hardest part is over with. And that's the part where you have to establish credibility.

Let your current customers refer you to possible prospects. Most of them would be happy to do it if you would ask them. Ask for referrals from people that can't use your product. Ask for referrals from people who don't even like you or your product. Get referrals from everyone. Don't be bashful.

Get a stack of referral letters from all of your satisfied customers. Ask your customers to call others on the telephone for you. Do whatever you need to do, but do it!

"Timid salesmen have skinny kids."   —JUDGE ZIGLAR

Day Nine

Sell to Your Existing Customers

Your best prospect for any product or service you have to offer is the customer you already have. Very few of us have penetrated our customer base thoroughly with all of our products and services.

If they currently are satisfied with using part of the product line, why wouldn't they be happy with the rest of the product line? Probably because you haven't asked them.

I believe this is one of the most overlooked markets: the existing customer. Yet this is the one who knows us and is the easiest to approach.

Always remember that your best prospect is your current customer.

Day Ten

Join a Leads Club

They are called many things: tips groups, leads clubs, networking groups and more. But they can help you more than you would believe.

A good networking group will have as its primary focus the generation of qualified business leads for its members. They normally only allow one member from any given industry to be in the group. The good ones require its members to provide leads for other members. They don't cost much to belong to. They usually meet either at breakfast or at lunch. They usually only last about an hour. They give you leads. If they are cost-effective and fit your schedule and give you leads, why wouldn't you want to belong?

So find a good one. Usually your Chamber of Commerce can provide you with a list of them. Visit as many as you can. When you find one that is dedicated to lead generation for its members, join. Then contribute all the leads you can. They will come back to you multiplied.

No one succeeds alone.   —RAY KROC

Day Eleven

Join an Association that Serves Your Industry

There are associations in every community that are made up of people you could do business with. Become involved.

First, join your own professional association. Become active. Become known as a mover and shaker in your industry.

Second, join other associations where there are large groups of users of your services. You may have to join as an affiliate or vendor. That's okay, join!

People do business with people they know. Get known by as many people as you possibly can.

Day Twelve

Learn from the Masters

Never stop learning. Some people say, "I've been doing this for twenty years, what's left to learn?" Plenty. You can never have too much information. So get more. Besides, do you have twenty years of experience or one year of experience repeated twenty times?

Learn from the masters. Read the books and listen to the tapes of Zig Ziglar, Brian Tracy, Mark Victor Hansen, Don Hutson, Larry Winget and others. These are people who have dedicated a lifetime of research to knowing what works and doesn't work in selling.

Be open to new ideas. Try new things. Try new ways of asking for the appointment or new ways of closing the sale. The masters study this stuff and teach this stuff and do this stuff every day. It will work if you work it!

Read *The Greatest Salesman In The World* by Og Mandino.

When you do the things of a master, your chances of becoming a master go way up!

Day Thirteen

Study Your Co-Workers

Study the actions of your co-workers. They may be coworkers in your office or salespeople in other businesses within your industry.

Look at their results. If they are doing something that works, do it. If they are doing something that doesn't work, don't do it. Sounds simple enough, doesn't it? It is.

Some of the greatest teachers in your life are sitting at the desk next to you. Some of your greatest teachers are your biggest competitors. Some of your greatest teachers are the biggest flops in your business. Pay attention! Learn from others' victories and their mistakes. Experience is the best teacher. Learn from someone else's experience as well as your own.

Be aware of others. Watch them, listen to them, study them.

Day Fourteen

Learn from the Winners in Unrelated Fields

You can learn from everyone. If you are in the insurance business, then try learning from someone in the banking business. In the telecommunications business? Try learning from someone in the medical industry. Don't become too narrowly focused in your pursuit of sales ideas and information.

Try to catch other companies and individuals in unrelated fields doing something right. Then figure out why it's working for them and try to repeat it in your business. Of course, it may require modification. But if it works in one business won't it work for you? I'll bet it will!

Be open. Be observant. Be risky. Look for good ideas everywhere.

Become a student of success!

Day Fifteen

Be Unique

Even though you are a student of the masters and of winners in your business and from other fields, that does not mean that you mimic them exactly.

Personalize everything. Make it yours. Add your uniqueness to every idea.

Think of the Diet Pepsi Uh-huh commercial. Do you think anyone else could do it quite like Ray Charles? Of course not. That commercial is Ray Charles. The same words by anyone else would bring in something totally different.

You have the same uniqueness. You have a style. If you don't know what it is, then ask someone to tell you. Then figure out how to add that style to everything you have learned.

Find your uniqueness and put it to use in all that you learn.

Day Sixteen

Believe

Believe in yourself. Know that you can do whatever you need to do and be whatever you need to be in order to have the results that you want to have. How you feel about yourself will directly impact your ability to sell your customer on you and your products.

Believe in your product. If you don't love your product so much that you would buy it if situations were reversed, then you need to find a new product.

Believe in your customer. Know that the customer is your boss. Believe that your success depends on satisfying your customer: the boss.

Believe in your company. Believe that your company has the best interest of the customer at heart. If they don't, then find a new company.

. . . all things are possible to those that believe!

—MARK 9:23

Day Seventeen

Want Everyone to Win

The goal of every sales person must be for the customer to win. Of course, the salesperson and the company should also win. There should be no losers when a sale is made.

Carry this another step. Want your competitors to win. That's right. The industry never benefits from the loss of any business. Cavett Robert says that we shouldn't be concerned about making our slice of the pie bigger, but that we should be concerned about making the pie itself bigger.

If we all make sure the customer wins, then there will be more than enough customers for all of us. There is a customer for every salesperson and for every company out there. There are plenty of customers to go around.

The more everyone wins, the more you will win.

Day Eighteen

Love Problems

Your ability to succeed in sales is based on your ability to solve the problems of other people.

Your compensation is based on your ability to solve the problems of others. If you solve lots of problems, then you get paid lots of money.

Problems are the basis for the existence of the company you work for. Your company provides products or services that solve certain problems. If it didn't, it wouldn't be in business.

You must do the same thing. You must provide solutions to the problems of your customer. When you become good at this, you will be more successful.

Problems determine your income, your employment, and your success! Learn to love problems!

Day Nineteen

Ask for the Business

We would all have more business if we would ask for more business. That's right. You don't have to be the best, you don't have to be the cheapest, you don't even have to be any good. All you've got to do is ask more.

We can all name probably a hundred examples of inferior products that are being sold all because someone asked someone else to buy them.

I'm telling you this stuff works! Just ask more people to do business with you and you'll do more business! I promise.

Ask everyone! Ask for bigger quantities. Ask for referrals. When they say "No" keep asking! Ask, ask, ask, ask, ask. Then ask again.

". . . ye have not because ye ask not."   —JAMES 4:2

Day Twenty

Learn to Walk

Walk away from some deals. Not all deals are good deals. There are some deals out there where there is no way for everyone to win. Avoid them. Walk.

An abusive prospect will be an abusive customer. Walk. A customer that pits you against your competitor in a price war will never be loyal to you. Walk. If a customer doesn't deal with you ethically, morally, honestly and with integrity, don't walk, RUN!

This is a tough one. It's requires skill and confidence. It is hard to learn when to do it and when to stay a little longer and see if the tide changes. But learn how to walk and get good at it. Otherwise, a mistake can be troublesome and costly.

There are some deals you should walk from.

Day Twenty-one
Say Thank You

This one is a biggy! Say thank you for everything and sincerely mean it. I can't tell you how thankful I am for every customer I have. I am thankful every time I get hired. I am thankful for everyone who buys one of my books or my tapes. I'll bet you are the same way.

The problem is not that we aren't thankful, it's that we don't say thank you. (By the way, thank you for buying this book!)

Say thank you in person. Say it in writing. Carry notes and postcards and drop your customers a note immediately! Make your thank you's personal and specific. Say thank you often.

Thank them for their time, their money, their business, for allowing you to see them, for taking your call, for being easy to do business with, for their hospitality, and the list goes on and on.

The more you are thankful for what you have, the more you will have to be thankful for.

—ZIG ZIGLAR

Day Twenty-two

Do What You Say You Are Going to Do

It is better to under-promise and over perform than to over promise and under-perform. Read it again.

If you do less than you have promised or less than you have said you are going to do then you have taken a major step in destroying the trust factor that is critical to the long term relationship you must establish with your customer in order to be more successful.

Do what you say you are going to do. Be there when you said you would. Mail it when you said you would. Deliver when you said you would. Call back when you said you would. Give them what you said you would. Got it? Do what you say you are going to do! Without exception. You can't afford to do any less.

Make sure that your words and your actions can be counted on.

Day Twenty-three

Do More Than You Say You Are Going to Do

This is the principle of Lagniappe. A Cajun/Creole term that means give the customer what they wanted, give them what they expected, give them what they bargained for, give them what they paid for, give them what you said you would, "and then some." Lagniappe means "and then some."

Lagniappe makes the difference. This is where you figure out ways to outperform yourself. It's fun, requires creativity, and is highly profitable. The salespeople and companies that become effective at this are the ones that get RICH!

There are no traffic jams in the extra mile.

Day Twenty-four

Do the Little Things

This will set you apart from the rest of the pack. The little things. And it's the little things that will sometimes have the biggest impact.

Write the thank you's that most people won't write. Call and tell your customers that you sincerely appreciate them and their business. Send birthday cards. Send notes on Secretary's Day to your customer's secretary. Just do the things that most people won't do. The little things!

Make just one more call every day. A little thing that will have big results. Get one percent better in everything you do. Anyone can do that, right?

Success does not come from doing extraordinary things. Success comes from doing the ordinary things extraordinarily well.

Day Twenty-five

Follow-Up

Don't bother making the first call if you're not willing to make the second, the third, the fourth and the fifth. Not everyone buys on the first call. You have to follow-up.

Follow-up to make sure that the customer is satisfied. I recently got a follow-up call to see if I was pleased with a $21 dollar rubber stamp! Was I impressed? You bet I was. So impressed that I bought another $50 worth of rubber stamps! Who won? We both did. Can't beat that, can you?

So follow-up is critical not only to the sales effort but to the customer service/satisfaction effort as well. And it's profitable!

Follow-up in writing, with a phone call and in person. Maybe all three. But regardless of how you do it, do it!

Day Twenty-six

Get a Picture Postcard

Have a high quality, black and white, friendly, smiling picture made of yourself. Then get three sayings, like: Thanks for your time! or Thanks for your business! or You're the best! or any other upbeat, appropriate sayings.

Then call a printer, give them your picture and the sayings and have three postcards made with the sayings on one side and your picture, name and address on the other. Make sure that you leave plenty of room to address it and write a short note on the picture side. Three cards can be laid out on an 8½ x 11 inch sheet of cardstock and the cost will be very low.

While your company may have their cards, you need your cards! They are personal and will have great meaning to your customers. Mail them out regularly for any and nearly every reason. Carry stamps with you so you can mail them immediately.

Follow-up is critical. Personalized, immediate follow-up is outstanding!

Day Twenty-seven

Be Stingy with Your Time

Nothing is more important than your time. Don't let anyone waste it. It is the only thing you can't get any more of and that you can never get back once it's gone. So be stingy with it.

Spend as much time as you can find talking with customers. This is your most important use of time.

Then spend as much time as necessary getting ready to talk to customers. Setting appointments. Preparing. Writing proposals, etc. But be careful. While this is important, it is not as important as actually talking with customers.

Then comes personal time. When you are on the job you don't have any of this. On the job, all of your time must be spent keeping existing customers, creating new customers and making yourself and your company the kind that people want to do business with. Anything else is a waste of time.

Your time is your most valuable asset.

Day Twenty-eight

Be GREAT on the Telephone

Not just good on the telephone. Good won't make you rich. Be GREAT on the telephone.

When you are on the telephone you have to sound better than you do in person. More enthusiastic, more friendly, more of everything. Why? Because they can't see you. They can only hear you and you have to be better than in person.

Record yourself when you are on the telephone. The device to do this is inexpensive and will quickly pay for itself. Listen to how you say things and what you say. Listen to yourself laugh and listen for how much you listen.

Then buy PhonePower, an audio program series and book by George Walther. His stuff is simply the best available.

The better you are on the telephone, the better your results will be.

Day Twenty-nine

Personal Hygiene

Sounds ridiculous to have to mention, but many don't mention it and they should. When you are a professional salesperson seeing and talking with people all day long, you are working! And you are up close to most of them. And you are extremely visible. How do you look? How do you smell?

Take special care with your fingernails, your breath, and with your deodorants and colognes and perfumes.

Carry stuff with you to help your breath (not chewing gum—very few people actually know how to chew it without being totally offensive).

And don't wear too much cologne or perfume. Too much is more offensive than none at all.

Everything about you should add to your presentation and not detract from it.

Day Thirty

Look Like a Million Buck$

Look as successful as you can possibly afford to. Your clothes, car and office should be monuments to your success. Look like a million bucks.

Some have said that you shouldn't drive big expensive cars. Your customers might think that you're making too much money from selling your products. How stupid! I want my salesperson to be successful. If they can afford to drive a big brand new Mercedes selling insurance than they must be really good at it. I want someone who's really good at it.

So look as good as you can afford to. Some rules: Wear expensive ties and shoes (and keep your shoes well shined). Ties and shoes also usually carry an outfit. Get your shirts starched. Carry an expensive pen. Carry a really good leather notepad and an expensive briefcase. Drive as nice a car as you can. People like to do business with winners! Look like a winner.

Your clothes, car, and office should be monuments to your success!

Day Thirty One

WOW! the Customer at Every Opportunity

Look for creative and fun ways to surprise your customer and WOW! them at every opportunity.

I once had a landlord stop by my offices in the middle of August with an ice cream truck. He brought everybody in my company out to the truck and bought us all ice cream bars. WOW!

Can you WOW! your customers? Sure you can. Get with your friends, your co-workers, your spouse, even your kids and think of ways to WOW! your customers.

WOW them with your service, your friendliness, your courtesy, your gratitude, your smile, your thoroughness, your efficiency, and your attitude.

Make'em say WOW!

CHAPTER 6

31 Days to Success!

Take Responsibility

This is where it all starts. No progress can be made in your life toward where you want to be until you first take responsibility for where you are. This is where the blaming stops and the finger pointing comes to an end. There can no longer be any excuses for why you aren't doing as well as you ought to be. You simply have to face yourself and take responsibility.

Take responsibility for where you are. Take responsibility for who you are. Take responsibility for what you have. Then make plans to move forward because now, maybe for the first time, you are ready to begin your journey of success.

"When you miss the target, never in history has it been the target's fault."   —UNKNOWN

Day Two

Make a Decision

Before you can go anywhere, you first have to know where you are and then make a decision to be somewhere else.

Make a decision right now to begin your journey toward becoming the best version of you that you can possibly be! And whatever you decide is fine, even if it's wrong. A bad decision is much better than no decision. At least you'll know quicker.

Charles "Tremendous" Jones says to make your decision and then work to make your decision right. That's a new twist for most of us but a great idea. You can't always make right decisions, so work hard to make any decision you do make, right.

"First you make your decisions, then your decisions make you."
—UNKNOWN

Day Three

Change

This is a tough one because change is never an easy task. We all get so comfortable doing things the way we do and thinking the way we do and talking the way we do, that to change and do it differently is difficult.

We have all formed habits of behavior that have determined where we are right now. These habits enslave us and it's necessary to break them and begin to do differently, think differently and talk differently. This isn't easy, but it is simple. The only way to change is to simply do it. That's all, just do it. No one can give you a magic formula for changing. No psychologist or scientist can explain the process. It just happens. You make a decision to be different and then just do it. So do it. You will never get different results by continuing the same behavior. That's insanity. So change.

"If you are going to change your life, you need to start immediately and you need to do it flamboyantly."

—WILLIAM JAMES

Day Four

Be Willing

Are you willing to do whatever it takes in order to get what you want? You have to be.

If you make a list of 10 things you have to do in order to get where you want and you are willing to do all but number 10, then don't bother starting on number 1. Because sure enough, number 10 will jump out of line and be right there in front of you. So when you make your list, make sure you are willing to do whatever it takes. That means the whole list.

But here is the good news. You are rarely asked to do whatever it takes. However, you are almost always asked to be willing to do whatever it takes. Be willing!

"The world is not made up of the have's and have-not's—but of the will's and will-not's."   —Unknown

Day Five

Have Vision

You need a vision for your life. A picture that you can create in your mind to see what you want to have, to picture yourself doing what you want to do and to visualize what you want to be.

Close your eyes and create little movies in your mind with you as the star and visualize your world the way you want it to be.

Napoleon Hill said, "Whatever the mind can conceive and believe, it can achieve."

Do this often. Create a vision for your life. Believe in your ability to achieve it, and it will happen for you.

"Whatever you vividly imagine, ardently desire, sincerely believe, and enthusiastically act upon must inevitably come to pass."
—PAUL J. MEYER

Day Six

Have Goals

You have to have goals if you want to be successful. Remember these rules for goal setting and achievement:

Make your goals big. Your goals should challenge you to be more, have more, do more, or give more.

Make your goals small. Have little-bitty goals that you can achieve to give you the confidence to achieve bigger ones. Besides, little goals are just big ones broken down into pieces.

Make your goals specific. Know exactly what you want to do, be or have.

Write them down. A goal not written down is a wish.

Review your goals often. Continually reinforce the specific direction for your life.

"Aim at nothing and you'll probably hit it."   —UNKNOWN

Day Seven

Start

After all is said and done, more is said than done. Setting your goals is important, and so is taking responsibility, and making a decision, but action makes things happen!

Get started. Don't wait. Things are not going to be any different for you until you start doing something different. What are you waiting for? For things to be "just right" before you start? For the timing to be perfect? For "all your ducks to be in a row?" This just isn't going to happen. Conditions are never going to be perfect. So don't bother waiting. You'll end up waiting forever. Just get started right now on your goal.

The best place to be when you start is where you are right now.

You don't have to be good to start, but you do have to start to be good.

Day Eight

Quit

In order to achieve greatness in your life there are some things that you simply must quit doing. Things like watching so much television, eating so much crummy food, hanging around with the wrong people, and on and on.

Here's a simple test to know whether you should quit something or not. Ask yourself the question, "Will this activity or relationship or thought move me closer to where I want to be?" If the answer is no, then quit it.

Very simple. Just understand that nothing is neutral. Everything either moves you closer or farther away from where you want to be. So quit everything that moves you farther away.

You are a reflection of what you see, what you hear, and the people you associate with.

Day Nine

Live With the Setbacks

Setbacks are going to happen. If you don't believe it, then you are naive. Everything good that you pursue will be challenged. That's just the kind of universe we live in. One of challenge. But that's good! When you are challenged, at least you will know you are on the right track.

So what do you do? Prepare for the challenges so you won't be surprised, then fight back against the challenges, then move on. Use the advice of my friend, Mark Victor Hansen. When you are faced with a challenge or rejection just use this four letter word: NEXT. Just say "next." This will keep you looking forward. You don't get farther down the road to success by looking backward. So say "next" and move on!

"Opportunity rarely looks like an opportunity. Often opportunity arrives incognito, disguised as misfortune, defeat, and rejection."
—DENIS WAITLEY

Day Ten

Stay

Persevere. Stay with it. Things are always changing. Give things time. Don't give up or quit too soon.

Understand that things don't always get better and that they often get worse. However, let a problem or challenge or setback run its course. Stay with it. Hang in.

How long should you stay? As long as you think you possibly can, and then just a little longer. Then when you are there, stay just a little longer. You can always stay longer than you expected.

Stay by increasing your ability to deal with things. Explore your options. Take action on several options. Seek professional advice. Give it your best. Give it time to work. Then if it doesn't, give yourself permission to let go and move on!

"Many of life's failures are men who did not realize how close they were to success when they gave up." —THOMAS EDISON

Day Eleven

Love Problems

Your ability to succeed is based on your ability to solve the problems of other people. Problems are the foundation of your success. Without problems you wouldn't have a job. Without problems your company wouldn't even exist. Your company provides products or services that solve certain problems. If it didn't, it wouldn't be in business.

Value is determined by the number of problems and the size of the problems you solve. In other words, you are paid in direct proportion to the problems you solve. So if you don't like how much you get paid, start solving bigger problems. Or start solving more problems of the size you are currently solving.

Your very being depends on problems. Without them you are, have and can do NOTHING. So learn to love them. And learn to solve them!

"Problems are the key to your significance."
—Mike Murdock

Day Twelve

Sell

You may say, "I'm not a salesperson!" I don't believe you. If you have a spouse, you are a salesperson. You sold your spouse on buying you didn't you? If you have kids, you are a salesperson. Don't you spend a good amount of time convincing them to see things your way? If you have a job, you are a salesperson. You had to sell that company on hiring you as an employee, didn't you?

Every day you spend a good portion of your time attempting to convince others to do it your way, to think your way, or to see it your way. That means you are a salesperson.

So get good at it. Regardless of what you do for a living, the better you are at persuading others, the more successful you will be. So get some books and tapes on sales. Study the principles and put them to work in your life.

"Nothing happens until something is sold."   —RED MOTLEY

Day Thirteen

Ask

You don't get much out of life that you don't ask for. Good things rarely interrupt you. You have to ask for them.

Ask your customers to buy more. Ask your employees to do more. Ask more from your company. Ask more from your family.

And most importantly, ask more from yourself! This is the real key. Ask what you can do to help. Ask what you have to offer. Ask what you can contribute. Ask how you can serve. Ask yourself how you can do more. Ask your spouse how you could be more helpful, loving or kind. Ask your kids what they would like you to be like. Ask your boss and employees how you could be more helpful. Ask your company how you could be a greater asset to them. Ask yourself what it would take to be and do your best.

". . . ye have not because ye ask not."   —JAMES 4:2

Day Fourteen

Be the Right Kind of Person

The kind of person you are is as important as any other principle of success. Because your doing is based on your being.

Be the kind of person that others trust, respect and enjoy being around. Be a person of integrity. Be known as honest and sincere. Your character is your most valuable asset.

Many studies have been conducted along these lines. They indicate that approximately 15 percent of your success is based on your technical skills and abilities. Only 15 percent! And 85 percent of your success is based on the kind of person you are, or your character. Focus on you first and skills second!

"Always do right . . . this will gratify some and astonish the rest."
                                                   —MARK TWAIN

Day Fifteen

Be Smarter

No matter how much you know, you need to know more. You simply can't succeed in the future with the information you currently possess. All of us must continue to get more information.

First, read more books. The average American reads only one book per year and they would be totally broke if they missed their next paycheck. You don't want to be like that. As a minimum, read one book per month. If you don't know what to read then call or write me and I'll send you a list of books to get started with.

Second, listen to educational audio programs. Start by listening in your car. Your radio isn't teaching you a thing and hasn't made you a dime! So use the time in your car for education!

"If you feed your mind as often as you feed your stomach, then you'll never have to worry about feeding your stomach or a roof over your head or clothes on your back."
—ALBERT EINSTEIN

Day Sixteen

Invest in Yourself

To read more and listen to audio programs means you are going to have to spend some money. How much money? How successful do you want to be? You decide.

You may say, "I'll just check the books out of the library." Not a good idea. Books need to be devoured. You have to underline and highlight and mark them up in order to really get all the good stuff, and libraries don't appreciate that. Buy the books.

Or you might say, "I've got a friend with some tapes, I'll just copy them." This is a no-no. Tapes are copyrighted. If you copy them you are breaking the law and are stealing from the author and the benefit you receive will be minimal if any! Buy the tapes!

"If a man empties his purse into his head, no one can take it away from him. An investment in knowledge always pays the best interest."
—BENJAMIN FRANKLIN

Day Seventeen

Be Enthusiastic

Enthusiasm is an essential ingredient for success. Let me give you some tips on how to become more enthusiastic:

Start every day by thinking enthusiastically. The way you begin your morning will set the mood for the entire day.

Look for the good in others and in situations. There is really a lot of good stuff to be excited about.

Surround yourself with enthusiastic people. Enthusiasm is contagious. Catch it from others.

Give your enthusiasm away. The more you give away the more you will have.

"Nothing great was ever achieved without enthusiasm."
—RALPH WALDO EMERSON

Day Eighteen

Smile

"Smile, it don't cost nothing." My dad said that to me nearly every day. He was right. It is one of the few things you can do that is free. And the benefits are enormous!

Smile and you will feel better about yourself. You will feel better about other people. Other people will feel better about you. The other person will feel better about himself or herself. Unpleasant situations can become neutralized. You will sell more. People will like being around you more.

"But, I don't feel like smiling." Do it anyway! Do it and maybe then you'll feel like it. And even if you don't, keep smiling! Remember, "An insincere smile is always better than a sincere frown."

"A smile is a gently curved line that sets a lot of things straight."
—ROBERT A. SCHULLER

Day Nineteen

Be Yourself

You might as well be yourself, because you can't be anyone else.

In all the world there is nobody exactly like you. Since the beginning of time there has never been anyone like you. And there never will be. Nobody has your eyes, your face, your voice or your personality. Nobody has your unique talents and abilities. Sure, some may be better at certain things than you, but none can be or do exactly like you. So celebrate! You are one of a kind.

If two people are exactly alike, one of them isn't necessary. This isn't the case. You aren't like anyone else. So be who you are. And be the best version of you that you can possibly be!

Celebrate your uniqueness!

Day Twenty

Lighten Up!

"You can live on bland food so as to avoid an ulcer; drink no teas or coffee or other stimulants in the name of health; go to bed early and stay away from night life; avoid all controversial subjects so as never to give offense; mind your own business and avoid involvement in other people's problems; spend money only on necessities and save all you can. And you can still break your neck in the bathtub, and it serve you right!"

—Eileen Gruder

"Blessed is he who has learned to laugh at himself, for he shall never cease to be entertained."   —John Powell

"A merry heart doeth good like a medicine . . .

—Proverbs 17:22

Day Twenty-one

Be Positive

This is your choice. You can choose to look at things positively or negatively. It is up to you. If you want to make more money, be happier, have lots of friends, have peace of mind and be more successful, then I suggest that you choose to be positive.

Having a positive attitude will not help you do anything better. However, it will help you do everything better than having a negative attitude will.

"But I have problems." We all do. Regardless of that fact, we can all choose our response to those problems and the attitude with which we approach those problems. Choose positively.

PMA = Positive Mental Attitude = Pays More Always

"Any fact facing us is not as important as our attitude toward it, for that determines our success or failure."
—Dr. Norman Vincent Peale

Day Twenty-two

Relax

I believe that you ought to work as hard as you can, play as hard as you can, and loaf as hard as you can.

The trouble is that we mix all of these together. We work while we play, or at least think about work while we play, which defeats the purpose of play. Or we play or loaf at work, which can cost us money and maybe our job.

The key is to give each area all you've got when you're doing it. So when you are relaxing, RELAX!

Discover the value of relaxation. Learn how to calm the mind, body and spirit. Then you'll have the energy to give play and work the energy they deserve.

"It is better to have loafed and lost than never to have loafed at all."
—JAMES THURBER

Day Twenty-three

Be Healthy

Sometimes people don't get started because they are truly too weak physically. Their mind is right, their attitude is right, they are enthusiastic, they believe, but they just don't have the physical energy to get going. Their "get-up-and-go has got-up-and-went!"

So get healthy. Stop eating foods that are bad for you. Lose weight if you need to. Take vitamins. Get a juicer and drink fresh fruit and vegetable juices to give you more energy and cure what ails you.

Start exercising. It's free. It doesn't cost a dime to go for a walk. Expense should never be an excuse for an unhealthy body.

Go to a doctor (a healthy, non-smoking, exercising doctor). Get a full physical and a plan for your physical health.

"To be rich and sick is stupid!"   —TOM HOPKINS

Day Twenty-four

Keep it in the Right Perspective

The way you see things is important to the quality of your life. Things will happen to you every day to help you lose your perspective. Situations will occur that will entice you to become petty, angry, picky and judgemental. Step back and put it in perspective. Is it really all that important? Will it really matter a week from now? Or even an hour from now?

Scope up.

Remember the purpose and vision for your life. Focus on the love in your relationships and leave the nagging to someone else. Remember that the angry customer or co-worker isn't really upset with you personally; they are just upset. The person that cut you off in traffic really wasn't out to get you specifically. Lighten up, scope up and move on!

"The essence of genius is knowing what to overlook."
—WILLIAM JAMES

Day Twenty-five

Go Big or Stay Home

This is about life-style! It's about flair! It's about pizzazz! It's about attitude!

It has nothing to do with money or what you have. It has everything to do with how you approach life and how you live it. It is a consciousness of prosperity. It is an attitude of abundance. It is believing in and enjoying what you have while you are on your way to having more. It is accepting and loving who you are, while on the way to being better. It is living life as an adventure. Go Big Or Stay Home is squeezing all of the life you can out of the little time you have.

"Life is too short to be little."   —DISRAELI

"Fortune favors the bold."   —VIRGIL

"Life is either a daring adventure or nothing at all."
      —HELEN KELLER

Day Twenty-six

Believe

Believe in what is right. Believe in what you do. Believe in other people. Believe in your company. Believe in your products and services. Believe in integrity. Believe in honesty, in justice and the truth. Believe in marriage. Believe in the family. Believe in democracy and all that it stands for. Believe in the future. Believe in opportunity and in possibilities. Believe in yourself. Believe in something bigger than yourself.

Your beliefs will determine your actions and your actions will determine your results. Therefore, your results are determined by your beliefs.

"If you can believe, all things are possible to him that believes."
—MARK 9:23

Day Twenty-seven

Be an Encourager

To encourage means "to put courage into." Just think of the good you could do in the universe if your goal was to put courage into people. What a service! Let me give you a few ways to encourage others:

Look people in the eye. Prove to them that they are worthy of your encouragement. Then smile at them!

Say thank you. Recognize and reward people for good behavior. Saying thank you is the easiest way.

Write notes of appreciation. It takes a minute, but words of encouragement written down mean more. You will be amazed at the impact a note will have on your spouse and kids!

Congratulate people in advance. Tell them that you believe in them, that you know they can do it, that they are winners!

"Unless life is lived for others, it is not worthwhile."
—MOTHER TERESA

Day Twenty-eight

Give

The principle of giving just can't be emphasized enough as a key principle to success.

"Nature abhors a vacuum." A scientific law of the universe that we all understand. It applies to you as well. There is no room for the good stuff to come into your life until you start making room for it by giving.

Give your time. Your time is the ultimate gift because when it's gone, it's gone! However, don't let this stand in the way of you giving away your money either. Give away some money. You'll know how much. Start with ten percent. You can move up from there.

Give joyfully! Nothing will ever you bring you more success and happiness than an unselfish gift.

"You give but little when you give your possessions, it is when you give of yourself that you truly give."   —KAHLIL GIBRAN

Day Twenty-nine

Know the Law
of Reciprocity

This Law says you are going to get back what you give; that life is reciprocal. Never doubt that this is a Law. It is. And don't bother trying to break it. The consequences can be catastrophic. It has been stated many ways:

"You can have everything in life you want if you will just help enough other people get what they want." —ZIG ZIGLAR

"Your rewards in life are in direct proportion to your service." —EARL NIGHTINGALE

For every action there is an equal and opposite reaction. —THE LAW OF CAUSE AND EFFECT

". . . for whatsoever a man soweth, that shall he also reap." —GALATIONS 6:7

What goes around, comes around.

Day Thirty

Be Balanced

Our lives have many areas: Career/Business, Social/Civic, Financial, Family, Physical/Health, Mental/Continuing Education, and Spiritual. To sacrifice any one of these areas would be to do your entire life a disservice.

Would you be a success if you made a million dollars and lost your health or your family? Absolutely not. So work hard to maintain balance in your life. It's not easy. Be aware. Ask your spouse or someone close to you to remind you now and then.

Give everything you have to everything you do. Give each area of your life your very best. And do something in every area of your life each day if at all possible.

"Success is being the best you can be in each area of your life without sacrificing the ability to be your best in each and every other area of your life." —LARRY H. WINGET

Day Thirty-one

Be Thankful

No matter how bad it may seem, it could always be worse. So be thankful. We are all so fortunate! You got up this morning and a lot of people didn't. Be thankful!

Start your day each morning by writing down five things you are thankful for. It can be things like your house, your car or the clothes you have to wear. Or things like your job, your friends, your boss or your customers. Certainly your list should include your family. But also have lists of little things. Things that you normally have taken for granted. Things like your comfortable chair or the sunshine, the rain, or the streets you walk or drive on. Things like your desk or radio or books. Or your knowledge, your ability to walk or to hear or speak.

We all have so much to be thankful for. Practice being thankful.

"The more you are thankful for what you have, the more you will have to be thankful for."
—ZIG ZIGLAR

www.ingramcontent.com/pod-product-compliance
Lightning Source LLC
Jackson TN
JSHW012130110225
78879JS00003B/6